PIZZA

A Slice of American History

LIZ BARRETT

Contributions from Lou Abate, Mark Bello,
Chef Santo Bruno, Roberto Caporuscio, Pat DePula,
Steve Green, Ruth Gresser, PJ Hamel, Jay Jerrier,
Brad Kent, Adam Kuban, Tom "The Dough Doctor" Lehmann,
Matt McClellan, Penny Pollack, Shawn Randazzo,
Peter Reinhart, Jesse Ryan, and Scott Wiener

Voyageur
Press

First published in 2014 by Voyageur Press, an imprint of Quarto Publishing Group USA Inc., 400 First Avenue North, Suite 400, Minneapolis, MN 55401 USA

Voyageur Press titles are also available at discounts in bulk quantity for industrial or sales-promotional use. For details write to Special Sales Manager at Quarto Publishing Group USA Inc., 400 First Avenue North, Suite 400, Minneapolis, MN 55401 USA.

To find out more about our books, visit us online at www.voyageurpress.com.

ISBN-13: 978-0-7603-4560-3

Barrett, Liz, 1974-
Pizza : a slice of american history / Liz Barrett.
pages cm
Includes bibliographical references and index.
ISBN 978-0-7603-4560-3 (sc)
1. Pizza. 2. Pizza–History. 3. Pizza–United States. I. Title.
TX770.P58B374 2014
641.82'480973–dc23

Editor: Grace Labatt
Design Manager: James Kegley
Cover designer: Diana Boger
Page designer: Amelia LeBarron
Cover photo: Rob Hammer Photography

Printed in China

10 9 8 7 6 5 4 3 2 1

DEDICATION

To pizza, without which this book would not be possible. And to Steve Green, my publisher at *PMQ Pizza Magazine*, who brought me into this amazing industry and allowed me the freedom to explore it as I saw fit. To my friends and loved ones, who stuck by me during the writing of this book, no matter how many times I had to cancel plans (pizza is on me next time, guys!). And to all of the hard-working pizza makers around the world, who dedicate their lives to bringing us joy with a simple slice of pizza.

CONTENTS

FOREWORD

My confidence was waning by the time we made our third illegal U-turn. Liz Barrett was behind the wheel, I was riding shotgun, and the GPS was probably just confused that we were trying to find yet another pizzeria—our third of the night. We were both in Orlando for a restaurant industry tradeshow, at which we had spent the entire day being bombarded with pizza. Yet here we were, following a hot lead into a sketchy part of town just to get some more. Such is the life of a pair of serious pizza enthusiasts who somehow managed to build careers out of obsession.

I first met Liz when she was the editor-in-chief of a pizza magazine based in Oxford, Mississippi. Yes, there is a pizza magazine—there are actually two in the United States—and subscriptions to both fed my own interest enough to help me launch a company that conducts tours of significant New York City pizzerias. Since 2008, Scott's Pizza Tours has introduced over twenty-five thousand people to the history and culture of the pizza capital of America. Running tours led me to gigs judging pizza competitions and emceeing at tradeshows across the country, and to appearances on just about every television network. I even published a book all about pizza box art, based on my collection of six hundred-plus boxes from forty-five different countries. I know that sounds made up, but it's all completely true. Such is the power of pizza.

Liz and I are far from alone. There's an entire subculture of pizza enthusiasts who spend their time investigating the nuances of what makes one pizzeria good and the other transcendent. They obsess over different oven types and sauce preparations, special methods of applying cheese, and ways of slicing a pizza. They debate the origins of significant pizza styles and what beverages best pair with them. They ask questions the average pizza eater doesn't think to ask.

Pizza is your passport to pizza obsession. It lays out a roadmap of pizza variations across the United States, with helpful hints for locating, identifying, consuming, and analyzing each manifestation. Thanks to her journalistic background, Liz Barrett digs deeper to explain the reasons for the various American styles, such as New York's thin, floppy slices and Chicago's hefty deep-dish. You'll even get recipes from some of the planet's most important pizza makers, so you can explore each style without leaving the safety of your kitchen.

This is the kind of book you'll have in the car for your first road trip to the great pizzerias of New Haven. It will accompany you on subway rides to New York's famous slice shops. You'll devour it again on your first flight to Naples. *Pizza* will escort you on your transition from casual pizza lover to all-out pizza geek.

As I learned in Orlando, Liz is the perfect companion when it comes to pizza adventuring. Just as she was literally willing to go the distance for great pizza (which we did eventually find), this book digs deep for slices of information about America's favorite import. Just be sure you're close to something saucy, cheesy, and crusty while reading it.

—Scott Wiener,
Scott's Pizza Tours, New York City

Lights shine their heavenly glow down on New York pizzas.

PIZZA FIRSTS

My first taste of pizza came one night during the mid-1980s, when my mom brought a pie home from a restaurant called The Wagon Wheel Saloon in Troy, Michigan. The restaurant is no longer there, but I still remember when that pizza arrived. The smell of Italian spices and melted cheese filled the house. We all gathered around and gobbled up every morsel until nothing was left but an empty box, scraped clean of any evidence.

Since then, I've eaten more pizzas than I can count, but I've never forgotten my first. I guess that's the way it is for most of us. I don't run into a lot of people who remember their first hamburger or taco, but most seem to remember their first pizza. Maybe it's because we usually have the experience while surrounded by friends and family, each hungrily grabbing a slice of the food that's inherently designed for sharing.

Twenty years after my first taste, I began working as a journalist for the pizza industry. Never could I have predicted that I'd be entrenched in pizza on a daily basis. Now, instead of just picking up my favorite pie from the corner pizzeria, I was interviewing pizzeria operators from all over the world, traveling near and far to see and experience

Pizza is serious business. Here's the judging table at a pizza competition, deciding who has the world's best pizza.

ferent types of pizza, and learning the where and when of how pizza started and how it continues to grow and evolve each year. Yeah, I was excited, to say the least.

Before then, pizza was just a fun food during a Friday movie night. While I loved eating it, I had never given a second thought to the people and history behind it. Meeting and talking to the men and women who have dedicated their lives to the craft of pizza-making has been such an eye-opening and heartwarming experience.

On the surface, pizza seems so simple, but when I started hearing stories of months—sometimes years—of experimentation to get a dough just right, of hand-built and imported ovens to impart the perfect bake, and of ingredients made or grown in-house in order to deliver the freshest taste possible, I knew pizza had a much larger story to tell. Seven years of being exposed to pizza on a daily basis have made me anxious to share some of the stories and pizzas I've learned about along the way.

I will always remember the story John Arena, co-owner of Metro Pizza in Vegas, shared with one of our pizza seminar groups a few years back. He spoke of when he was a young boy growing up in New York and his dad

would come home from working at the pizzeria. He said that when his dad would come into his room to kiss him goodnight, he always smelled like pizza. And so from an early age, John always associated pizza with love.

The most successful pizzeria operators I've spoken with always have a common love of and passion for what they're doing. You can taste it in the finished product. I equate it with being able to taste a mother's love in Sunday supper. Even though you may not know the pizza makers by name,

Metro Pizza pies.

Joe has a pizza going out the
window. Is it coming to you?
Photo courtesy of Aurelio's Pizza

Photo courtesy of Aurelio's Pizza

A Margherita pizza similar to the one Raffaele Esposito would have served to Queen Margherita. This one is found at Spacca Napoli in Chicago.

A name used for a pizza maker, a **PIZZAIOLO** usually works with an Italian-style, wood-burning oven. Other similar terms include *pizzaioli* (plural) and *pizzaiola* (female).

you know they are creating something for you, using dough they've mixed and kneaded with their hands, sauce with spices they've hand-selected, cheese that's often hand-grated. It's a true labor of love, and they get no greater pleasure than from watching you enjoy it. It's for that reason that you won't find many recipes in this book. The recipes you *will* find are

The mid-century pizza explosion hit Times Square in New York, seen here in 1958. *Associated Press*

included solely to give you an idea of how each style is created. I'd much rather you experience each pizza in a place that can also help you enjoy the history behind its pie.

A LITTLE PIZZA HISTORY

With more than seventy thousand pizzerias in America, pizza has become so familiar that it's sometimes difficult for us to imagine a time when it didn't exist. But the reality is, before the 1950s, most people in America had never seen or heard of "pizza." Once the masses got wind of it, however, the floodgates opened. The industry exploded, with pizza shops—both mom-and-pops and chains—churning out pies, while manufacturers set out to create pizza mixes and frozen pizzas for busy house-wives to prepare at home. The industry, and our growing consumption of pizza, has not waned since.

You're probably wondering how we didn't notice earlier something that today is so much a part of our lives. The fact is that pizza has been in America since the late 1800s, when Italian immigrants brought their recipes with them through Ellis Island. So what gives?

Well, to fully tell the story, let's go back to just prior to when Italians arrived in America. Then we'll fast forward to the present day.

Many historians refer to Neapolitan pizza chef Raffaele Esposito's preparation of a pizza for Queen Margherita of Savoy in 1889 as one of pizza's first big appearances. But other records have pizza dating back as far as the sixth century BC—during long marches, soldiers led by Persian king Darius the Great baked flatbreads covered with cheese and dates on their battle shields. In 79 AD, under the

The ladies gather in the kitchen to make pizza during the 1940s at Pizzi Café in Conneaut, Ohio.
Photo courtesy of Pizzi Café

ashes of the Mount Vesuvius eruption, evidence was found in Pompeii and Neopolis (the Greek colony that would later become Naples) of shops that looked like what we now know as pizzerias, and of a flat cake resembling pizza.

In the sixteenth century, a full three hundred years before Queen Margherita took her first bite of pizza, Neapolitans were enjoying tomato-topped pies. And in the seventeenth century, anyone who ventured into the poorer sections of Naples could sample the popular peasant food that was served up out of tin stoves, balanced on the heads of *pizzaioli* (pizza chefs). In 1738, the now-famous Antica Pizzeria Port'Alba opened shop

as a stand for the peddlers who had been cooking their pizzas in wood ovens and keeping them warm in tin stoves. The resulting restaurant in Naples, which still stands today, opened its doors in 1830.

So, you may be wondering why Queen Margherita's pizza party stands out in history, when Italians had already been eating pizza for so many years. Yes, she was a queen, but she certainly wasn't the first queen to eat pizza.

You might say that some savvy promotional know-how of one Raffaele Esposito helped make a mark on pizza history that day. Esposito, who was the owner of a pizzeria now known as Pizzeria Brandi in Naples, decided to create three unique pizzas for the queen, including one he must have known she'd enjoy. When Queen Margherita chose his pizza topped with tomatoes, mozzarella, and basil—representing the colors of the Italian flag—as her favorite, Esposito renamed it the "Pizza Margherita." It was an instant hit—so much so that we're still calling this pizza by its famous name more than a hundred years later.

Pizza arrived in the States in the late 1800s in much the same way—it was confined to the homes and neighbor-hoods of Italian-Americans and sold to laborers who needed an easy and inexpensive lunch. It went for decades virtually unnoticed by everyone else.

Some say that it was the soldiers returning from World War II with a new craving for Italian food that spurred the pizza craze. Others argue that many soldiers weren't exposed to pizza while stationed overseas, so it was the advent of new oven technology and grocery pizza that helped pizza's expansion. Still others say it was the promotion of pizza by celebrities, such as Frank Sinatra, Sophia Loren, and Dean Martin, that spurred America's love of pizza. (Remember Dean

"When the moon hits your eye like a big pizza pie, that's amore."

—Lyricist Jack Brooks

Martin's popular, pizza-referencing song "That's Amore," from 1953?)

While experts may never agree on some of pizza's big turning points, this book will explore how, over the last one hundred years, pizza has gone from virtually nonexistent in America to our nation's favorite food, by adapting its form and ingredients to each region's needs and wants. History has shown that almost every culture has made modifications to foods adopted from other nations, in order to make them work with available ingredients and equipment. Pizza is no exception. A bit of redesign may have occurred to the traditional Neapolitan pizza, but with today's access to Italian ingredients and equipment, we now see many pizza chefs returning to the early techniques of pizza-making, all in an effort to give your taste buds a story to tell.

In *Pizza*, we'll discover how popular pizza styles in America have put their own unique spin on an Italian classic.

Some chapters will also provide a short list of pizzerias located outside of the specialized style's typical region, as these may be closer to you. After all, you'll want to try every style. We'll also go below the surface to discuss pizza crust, cheese, toppings, sauces and spices, the ovens used to cook your favorite pies, and more. And just when you thought you knew everything there was to know about pizza, we'll explore how chains and technology have affected pizza's growth in America, and how pairings and the diet revolution continue to take pizzeria menus in new directions. By the time you're finished, you should feel like you've discovered the ultimate pizza manual, with everything from history to industry lingo to the inner workings of how it all comes together behind the scenes.

The pizza industry is filled with thousands of passionate people who have helped to make this industry what it is today. Find interviews with a few of them throughout the book, under the heading Living the Pie Life. Throughout pizza's storied history, one thing has remained constant, and that's the love that goes into each pie, whether from an Italian grandmother making pizza for her family, a chef creating a custom pizza for his customers, or you baking a pizza with the help of friends and family. It's easy to understand why pizza is America's favorite comfort food, and why it continues to create memories that last a lifetime.

Enjoying a slice at De Lorenzo's Tomato Pies in Trenton, New Jersey.
Photo courtesy of De Lorenzo's

Penny Pollack

Penny Pollack is a pizza lover, the co-author of *Everybody Loves Pizza*, and the dining editor for *Chicago* magazine.

We can't show you what Penny looks like— she must be able to judge pizzas (and other food) anonymously. Instead, here's a nice photo of Chicago. *Spirit of America/Shutterstock.com*

As the dining editor for *Chicago* magazine, you report on all types of food. What inspired you to co-author a book about pizza in 2005?
It was simple. The publishers called me. I was flattered that they turned to Chicago instead of New York for a pizza book.

How did writing *Everybody Loves Pizza* help your own love for pizza grow?
It was such a great experience and my husband was so supportive. We didn't have much of a budget for the book. We traveled to pizzerias around the country (on the pretense of visiting friends), conducted a ton of research online, and looked to college towns and government hubs for additional information. For the recipe chapter, some people told us that their recipes were a deep, dark secret they kept in a lockbox, while others gave of them freely. Lombardi's in New York took photos right off their walls for us. The backstories were just fabulous. I've always loved pizza, but I have a really warm feeling about it now.

What style of pizza do you like?
I like all three of the styles we have in Chicago: Chicago thin, deep-dish, and Neapolitan.

Do you have a favorite pizza memory?
Our grandchildren were sleeping over and, of course, we were going to go out for pizza. However, they both wanted something different—our granddaughter, Annie, wanted Giordano's, and our grandson, Will, wanted Pizano's. We had them choose a number between one and ten. Annie won. Will said, "Do over!" but we made him play by the rules. So we headed to Giordano's, but when we got there, the place was closed. When we decided to go to Pizano's, Will fell to his knees, raised his arms and yelled, "Yes!" Annie, upset that she couldn't have Giordano's, said that she wasn't going to eat, but she quickly changed her mind when the pizza arrived.

How do you feel pizza has changed over the past five to ten years?
Pizza has become chic, sophisticated, and pricey. It's a whole new ball game; the global outlook has grown. Now you don't have to go to a pizzeria for a pizza. You can go to almost any joint—from newfangled gastropubs to bistros to diners—because everyone is doing something related to pizza.

When people outside of Chicago think of Chicago pizza, they usually think of deep-dish, but what does the current Chicago pizza landscape really look like?
Tourists definitely go for the deep dish; Chicago invented it in the 1940s, and it's been a foodie icon here ever since. But Chicago-style thin crust is also popular. What has captivated us lately is Neapolitan-style pizza. New, hip trattorias make wood-burning ovens the center of their dining rooms and bake pizzas with blistered collars and fresh, simple toppings. It took a while to catch on because Chicagoans love both their deep-dish and cracker-crust traditions. Neapolitan is neither, so it wasn't immediately accepted.

17

ABOVE: Neapolitan-style pizza from Olio Pizza e Più in New York City.

LEFT: Naples, 1904. *Library of Congress*

NEAPOLITAN
AND NEW YORK STYLE

NEAPOLITAN-STYLE PIZZA

How to Recognize It

Small in size (around eleven inches in diameter); prepared in a wood-burning oven that produces light to dark charring on the crust; minimal toppings; more sauce than cheese; sometimes served uncut in the traditional Naples style.

Where to Find It

Originally hailing from Naples on the west coast of Italy, the Neapolitan style has experienced a resurgence in America over the past couple of decades. It's now easily found in pizzerias across the country.

We have countless styles of pizza to choose from today, but the very first style introduced to America was a version of the Neapolitan pizza, brought over from Naples, Italy, in the late 1800s. Italians had already been enjoying our favorite food since the early 1800s—Naples' first pizzeria, Antica Pizzeria Port'Alba, began peddling pies from a small stall in 1830.

In the early days of American pizza, Italian immigrants did not have access to wood-burning ovens, so America was first introduced to a slightly altered version of Neapolitan pizza, cooked using coal. It wasn't until many years later, in the 1980s, that pizza makers decided to return to the traditional Italian method of baking pizzas in wood-fired ovens. We were thus introduced to the original Neapolitan style.

Today, to be considered truly Neapolitan according to the Associazione Verace Pizza Napoletana (AVPN)—a group of Neapolitan pizza makers formed in 1984 that has certified nearly one hundred American pizzerias as "authentic Neapolitan"—pizzerias must meet strict guidelines, including the use of a 900-degree Fahrenheit wood-burning oven; fresh ingredients, preferably imported from the Campania region of Italy or the region's capital, Naples; hand-working of the dough; and a finished pizza no larger than eleven inches in diameter.

The **AVPN** stands for the Associazione Verace Pizza Napoletana, or the True Neapolitan Pizza Association, a nonprofit organization formed in 1984 in Naples to promote and protect true Neapolitan pizza.

Spacca Napoli in Chicago has been certified as a true Neapolitan pizzeria by the Associazione Verace Pizza Napoletana.

Not all pizzerias with wood-burning ovens have been certified as authentic Neapolitan, but those that have not can still produce some pretty spectacular pies, with the wood helping to deliver a smoky flavor and the high heat producing a crispy, lightly charred bottom. An increasing number of pizzerias each year introduces this Neapolitan style, and with its gourmet appeal and petite size, the pizzas are savored by pizza lovers from big cities to small towns across the United States.

There are two official types of Neapolitan pizza, according to the AVPN: marinara, with tomato, oil, oregano, and garlic; and Margherita, which has tomato, oil, *mozzarella di bufala* (water buffalo's milk mozzarella) or *fior di latte* (cow's milk mozzarella), and basil.

Ingredients are everything when it comes to creating a true Neapolitan pizza. The crust begins with 00 flour, a very finely ground Italian flour, which helps to produce a highly digestible crust. The sauce is created with San Marzano tomatoes from the Campania region of Italy, where nearby Mount Vesuvius produces minerals in the soil. The basil must be fresh, and the olive oil extra-virgin.

So why these ingredients?

San Marzano tomatoes have been highly regarded for their superior taste for more than a hundred years. They appear similar in size to a Roma tomato, but the inner flesh is thicker and there are fewer seeds. The taste is both strong and sweet. While the seeds can grow anywhere, the sweetest San Marzanos come from the Campania region.

Pizza used to be regarded as a food for the poor. Ingredients and toppings had to be minimal and easily accessible. A simple marinara pizza could be made with flour on hand and tomatoes, oregano, and garlic from the garden. And with so many olives growing in Italy, it wasn't unusual for pizza makers to produce their own olive oil as well.

When it came to cheese, Italians only had to look as far as the domesticated water buffalo, which they were already using for milk. Buffalo milk mozzarella

00 FLOUR (double zero flour) is a highly refined, ultra soft, high-protein flour from Italy that is used by most Neapolitan-style pizza makers.

Tribecca Allie Café in the small town of Sardis, Mississippi, has won national acclaim for its Neapolitan-style pizzas, cooked in a wood-burning oven built by the owner.

is considered to be creamier and more flavorful than cow's milk because of its higher fat content.

Neapolitan-style pizzerias that choose to serve the style without certification from the AVPN have free rein to top their pizzas with a plethora of gourmet ingredients ranging from specialty meats to regional cheeses, unique sauces (such as béchamel,

(continued on page 26)

"Neapolitans have always had their fast food. It's called pizza."

—Film director Luciano De Crescenzo

HOW TO MAKE IT

Although it's impossible to mimic a 900-degree Fahrenheit wood-burning oven at home, you can still create a very good imitation of a classic Neapolitan-style pizza. Try this one from Ruth Gresser, the owner and chef at Pizzeria Paradiso/Birreria Paradiso in Alexandria, Virginia. The following recipes—including descriptions—were excerpted from *Kitchen Workshop: Pizza*, by Ruth Gresser, © Quarry Books, 2014.

Neapolitan-Style Pizza Dough

Plan ahead when making this soft, supple dough, as it requires two slow rises. It will take at least 16, and up to 48, hours from beginning to end. I suggest making the dough in the morning of day one and serving the pizza for dinner the following day, with one rise at room temperature and the other in the refrigerator. Weigh the water for this recipe to ensure accuracy. You can order Type "00" flour online if you find it hard to locate in local stores.

Makes dough for two 12-inch pies

12 oz. warm water

1/4 tsp. fresh compressed yeast

1 lb. Type "00" flour

1 tbsp. sea salt flakes *

*If you cannot locate sea salt flakes, you can substitute 2 tsp. medium-ground sea salt or kosher salt.

Instructions

Place the water in the bowl of an electric mixer. Whisk the yeast into the water. Stir in 4 oz. of the flour. Let stand for 1 hour. In a separate bowl, mix together the remaining flour and the salt. Place the bowl with the yeast mixture onto the mixer and fit with a paddle attachment. With the mixer on the lowest speed, add the flour and salt mixture slowly (¼ c. at a time) until all of the flour is incorporated. Mix for about 2 minutes after each addition of flour.

Replace the paddle with the dough hook and knead the dough for 3 minutes on the lowest speed. Increase the speed to medium and continue kneading for 10 minutes or until the dough is smooth, elastic, and easily comes off the side of the bowl. Cover the bowl with plastic wrap and let the dough rise for 8 to 10 hours at room temperature, or up to 24 hours in the refrigerator.

Turn the dough out onto a floured surface. Cut into 2 equal pieces. Sprinkle each piece of dough with flour and lightly

The **DOP** (Denominazione di Origine Protetta or Protected Designation of Origin) and **DOC** (Denominazione di Origine Controllata or Controlled Designation of Origin) are Italian laws passed in the 1950s. These guarantee that the food and wine marked Italian really came from the region claimed (look for the symbols DOC and/or DOP on labels).

flour your hands. If your dough is tacky, use a generous amount of flour when shaping the balls of dough. Shape each piece into a ball.

Place the dough balls on a floured plate and cover it with plastic wrap. Let them rise for either 6 hours at room temperature, up to 24 hours in the refrigerator, or until double in size. This is a soft dough that tends to spread when it rises. It may resemble a flattened ball at the completion of the rise. (At this point, the dough may be frozen. When ready to use, thaw overnight in the refrigerator.) Allow refrigerated dough to stand at room temperature for 1 hour before using.

San Marzano Tomato Sauce

This simple sauce is good any time of year, and qualifies under the "True Neapolitan" pizza guidelines. You can make this sauce with fresh tomatoes, but only the San Marzano tomato meets the DOC guidelines. Makes 1 ½ cups

2 c. drained, canned whole San Marzano tomatoes (about one 28 oz. can)

½ tsp. olive oil

¼ tsp. (or to taste) sea salt flakes

Instructions

Pass the tomatoes through the medium blade of a food mill or a medium strainer into a mixing bowl. Stir in the olive oil and salt. Store the sauce in the refrigerator for up to three days or freeze for longer storage.

The Neapolitan

The ingredients for this pie make it as close to a "True Neapolitan" pie as you can get from your home oven. To fully qualify, you'd need to install a wood-burning oven and cook at heats upwards of 905 degrees Fahrenheit.
Makes one 12-inch pie

1 ball Neapolitan-style pizza dough

Cornmeal, for sprinkling

1/3 c. San Marzano tomato sauce

3 oz. fresh buffalo mozzarella, torn into 10 to 12 pieces

Sea salt flakes to taste

Olive oil, for drizzling

Instructions

Place a pizza stone on the top rack of a cool oven. Set the oven to broil and preheat for 30 minutes.

On a floured counter, flatten the ball with your fingertips and stretch it into a 12-inch round. If your dough is tacky, use a generous amount of flour when forming the pizza round.

Sprinkle a pizza peel with cornmeal and lay the pizza dough round on it. Spread the tomato sauce onto the pizza dough, leaving ½ to ¾ inch of dough uncovered around the outside edge. Arrange the cheese on top of the tomato sauce. Sprinkle with salt and drizzle with oil.

Give the peel a quick shake to be sure the pizza is not sticking to it. Slide the pizza off the peel onto the stone in the oven. Broil for 1½ minutes, then turn the oven temperature to the highest bake setting and cook for 4 minutes. Quickly open the oven door, pull out the rack, and, with a pair of tongs, rotate the pizza (not the stone) a half turn. Cook 4 to 5 minutes more.

Using a pizza peel, remove from oven. Cut into slices and serve.

NEAPOLITAN'S SECOND COUSIN: NEW YORK STYLE

How to Recognize It

Big, wide slices that often need to be folded in order to eat them; hand-tossed crust made with high-gluten bread flour; light sauce; sometimes heavy cheese; ordered by the slice or by the whole pie.

Where to Find It

If you want a real New York slice, it's best to grab one in New York. There are some great New York-style pies in New Jersey as well. Comparable slices can be found around the country, but nothing tastes quite the same as eating a slice on the streets of New York. Call it the water, the air, the mood; whatever the reason, a New York-style slice is just best in New York.

(continued from page 22)

Alfredo sauce, and garlic sauce), and vegetables (including Brussels sprouts, potatoes, and cauliflower). The wood-burning oven imparts a delicious, smoky flavor to almost anything a pizza chef can dream up.

Almost immediately after Italians began immigrating to America, New York-style pizza was introduced. Pizza in Naples had always been cooked in wood-burning ovens, but in early-twentieth-century America, it

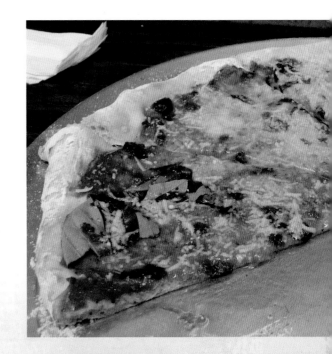

Pizzas at Di Fara in Brooklyn, New York, are so popular that lines are known to wrap around the building any day of the week, while owner Domenico DeMarco handcrafts each and every pie.

SECRETS OF PIZZA

Did you know that there's a man in Manhattan, Kansas, they call the "Dough Doctor"? Tom Lehmann is a virtual encyclopedia of dough knowledge who has been working with pizza for the American Institute of Baking since 1967. He writes and speaks regularly on the topic of creating the perfect pizza dough and is called upon to provide technical assistance to manufacturers and pizzerias that are having dough issues.

Tom Lehmann, the "Dough Doctor," in action.

was more economical to burn coal than wood. When Gennaro Lombardi opened his pizzeria in present-day Little Italy in 1905 and decided to use a coal oven, his departure from the traditional Naples style pioneered the New York style that continues to flourish today.

In fact, all pizzerias used coal-fired ovens until after World War II. The huge shift in the industry came when soldiers began returning from Italy with a craving for the pizzas they had enjoyed so much overseas. One of those soldiers, Ira Nevin, had experience in oven repair. He created the first gas-fired oven in 1945, changing the pizza scene forever by

speeding up the baking process and making it cleaner, cheaper, and more efficient. Pizzerias with gas-fired ovens quickly spread from New York to every other part of the country over the next twenty years.

RIGHT: Little Italy, New York, in 1908. *Library of Congress*

NEAPOLITAN AND NEW YORK STYLE

> **"I talked to a calzone for fifteen minutes last night before I realized it was just an introverted pizza."**
>
> — *Author Jarod Kintz*

Antonio Totonno Pero worked for Lombardi's in 1905 and later opened Totonno's on Coney Island. Both pizzerias are still very popular with locals and tourists.

PIZZA IN THE MOVIES

It's hard to watch a movie and *not* see pizza nowadays. You can practically place a bet on pizza making a cameo appearance at some point during the flick. Here's a short list of pizza's big-screen appearances over the years. Can you recall the pizza scenes in each of the following movies?

1. *A Nightmare on Elm Street 4: The Dream Master* (1988): What undesirable topping was found on Freddy Krueger's pizza?

2. Robert De Niro punches a pizza in what 1970 comedy?

3. *Back to the Future Part II* (1989): What popular pizza brand was shown in the scene where a tiny pizza grew large in the microwave?

4. *Die Hard* (1988): Finish the sentence: "Do I sound like I'm _____ a pizza?"

5. *Do the Right Thing* (1989): Why does the character Buggin' Out want to boycott Sal's Pizza?

6. *Dodgeball* (2004): Ben Stiller was showing a little too much love for pizza in this scene. What was he caught doing?

7. *Dog Day Afternoon* (1975): What is Al Pacino doing in this movie when he orders a pizza?

Just learning about Cuba, and having some food. © Moviestore Collection Ltd / Alamy

8. *E.T.* (1982): What popular game was being played when a pizza order was placed?

9. *Eat Pray Love* (2010): At which famous Italian pizzeria does Julia Robert's character dine?

10. *Fast Times at Ridgemont High* (1982): This actor shot to fame after the popular scene in which his character receives a pizza delivery during class. Name the star.

11. *Goodfellas* (1990): Something other than pizza went into the oven. What was it?

12. *Home Alone* (1990): What's the name of the pizzeria that delivers to Kevin when he's home alone?

13. *House IV* (1992): A truly scary pizza! What kitchen equipment is used in an attempt to "kill" the pie?

14. *Loverboy* (1989): What type of costume does a young Patrick Dempsey wear for his pizzeria job?

15. *Saturday Night Fever* (1977): How many slices does John Travolta order in the opening scene, which takes place in Brooklyn?

16. *Spaceballs* (1987): What was the name of the character who looks like a giant pizza?

17. S*pider-Man 2* (2004): With the help of some strategically placed webs, how many blocks was Spiderman able to travel in order to deliver his pizza on time?

18. *Star Trek IV: The Voyage Home* (1986): What is Captain Kirk's beverage of choice with his pizza?

19. *The Gold of Naples* (1954): What does Sophia Loren's character claim must have gotten lost in the pizza dough?

20. *The Goonies* (1985): What pizza topping does the felon say they're going to kill each other over?

For answers, see page 170.

Tomato pie at De Lorenzo's Tomato Pies in Trenton, New Jersey. The pizzeria moved to Robbinsville, New Jersey, in 2012.

CHAPTER TWO

TOMATO PIE

TOMATO PIE

How to Recognize It

Depending on what region you're in, there are several different types of pizza referred to as "tomato pie." There's a "reverse" pizza, which is a basic pizza but with the placement of sauce and cheese reversed (round or square); a Philly tomato pie, a thick, square, room-temperature pizza found at bakeries and topped with a thick sauce (or "tomato gravy") and a sprinkling of Parmesan or Romano cheese (square); and a hand-tossed dough topped with tomato sauce, oregano, olive oil, and a dusting of cheese (usually round). What you'll notice with all tomato pies is that the sauce is the star of the show. Tomato sauce sometimes slips by unnoticed in pizzas that are topped with lots of cheese and other ingredients. Not so in tomato pies, which proudly present their sauce front and center.

Where to Find It

The reverse pizza, as it is often referred to, is most often found in New Jersey and certain areas of New York. The Philly tomato pie can be found in Philadelphia, some parts of central New York, and south New Jersey. The hand-tossed tomato pie is usually spotted in New Haven, Connecticut.

It's been rumored that the tomato pie was conceived in Naples, when some Italian bakers were making bread one day and decided to put tomatoes on it prior to baking. Others say the Philly tomato pie was created when bakers threw a bunch of leftover hoagie rolls into a greased pan and put thick tomato sauce on top of them. Regardless of how each pie originated, it's still popular today because of its delightfully simplistic mix of ingredients, which usually includes a hearty tomato sauce, oregano, olive oil, garlic powder, and Romano cheese.

The name "tomato pie" may have sprung from an attempt to simplify the Italian word "marinara" for Americans. In Italy, the most traditional types of pizza were marinara (tomato sauce, olive oil, oregano, and garlic) and Margherita (tomato sauce, cheese, olive oil, and basil). In the early twentieth century, most Americans probably wouldn't have understood what a "marinara pie" was. "Tomato pie" worked best for menu and advertising purposes until "pizza pie"—and eventually "pizza"—caught on.

The "reverse pizza" tomato pie first came on the scene in 1910 at Joe's Tomato Pies in Trenton, New Jersey. Joe Papa, who had immigrated to the Trenton neighborhood of Chambersburg from Naples in the early 1900s, worked at Joe's before opening his own pizzeria, Papa's Tomato Pies,

in 1912, when he was just seventeen. Reverse pizzas are similar to traditional pizzas, but shredded mozzarella goes on first and a healthy helping of crushed tomatoes tops it off. Another big name in tomato pies, DeLorenzo's Tomato Pies, which opened in 1936, also arrived in New Jersey via Naples. DeLorenzo's creates its pies in a similar way. I visited Papa's and DeLorenzo's on the same day a few years back. The nostalgia of both pizzerias was felt throughout the buildings and in the pizzas. As a tomato lover, I appreciated

A tomato pie at Papa's Tomato Pies in Trenton, New Jersey, before the pizzeria moved to Robbinsville, New Jersey, in 2013.

EXTRA TOPPING

As if making pizza weren't fun enough, there's a United States Pizza Team comprised of a group of pizza makers who travel the globe making pizzas and competing in acrobatic dough-spinning competitions.

ABOVE: Jimmy DeLorenzo in front of the shop in the late 1930s. *Photo courtesy of DeLorenzo's*

RIGHT: Owner Gary Amico makes a pie at DeLorenzo's.

the ability to taste the tomato sauce before the cheese in every bite.

Around the same time that Papa's opened, a baker from Naples, Eugeno Burlino, was selling his own version of tomato pies—made by his wife—for a nickel on the streets of Utica, New York, to supplement his income as a pastry chef. The pies were simple: dough, sauce, and Romano cheese, or olive oil and anchovy. People who wanted a pie would call out to Burlino, "Hey, *scugnizzi*," which meant "street urchins" or "street kids." The pies' popularity led Burlino to open O'Scugnizzo Pizzeria in 1914.

While Neapolitan immigrants were creating their own style of tomato pies in New Jersey and New York, another version was taking shape in Philadelphia, with the help of Sicilians.

The Philly tomato pie, most commonly found in bakeries in the Norristown area of Pennsylvania, dates back to 1910, when it had its origins at places such as Iannelli's Bakery in Philadelphia. These pies are cooked on a square baking sheet and eaten at room temperature; they are most closely related to baked focaccia breads (think of a Sicilian pie without the cheese). The popular Conshohocken Bakery in Conshohocken, Pennsylvania, describes its tomato pie as "an 18-inch x 25-inch sheet of dough with homemade tomato sauce spread generously on top and baked; the cheese, garlic powder, and oil are added after baking."

TOP: O'Scugnizzo owner Eugeno Burlino with his portable pizza oven in 1954.
Photo courtesy of O'Scugnizzo Pizzeria
BOTTOM: Terry Iannelli mans the oven at Iannelli's Bakery in Philadelphia, Pennsylvania.
Photo courtesy of Iannelli's Bakery

And finally, the New Haven tomato pie made its debut at Frank Pepe Pizzeria Napoletana in 1925. This pizza is topped with tomato sauce, garlic, oregano, olive oil, and grated cheese, similar to the Philly tomato pie. But this pizza has a thin crust, unlike the thick, focaccia-like crusts of Philadelphia, and is served piping hot from a coal-burning oven.

Back when pizza first came to America, there were no such things as "deluxe" pizzas or the gourmet toppings we see today. We enjoyed simple, fresh food that had a minimalistic quality. Pot roast and potatoes were the norm for most family suppers, and no one complained about a lack of variety in his or her diet. So tomato pies, while they may seem simple to us nowadays, were unique and quite fascinating when they were first introduced to America.

The fact that the tomato sauce is highlighted means that great care must go into choosing the tomatoes and/ or sauce for a tomato pie. Many pizza makers crush their own homegrown tomatoes, while others go through months of trial and error to perfect a sauce that will provide great tomato flavor but isn't too acidic, sweet, or salty. Because of this ultimate goal of reaching tomato perfection, once you taste a tomato pie for yourself, any previous adoration you held for tomatoes is sure to increase threefold.

Tomato pie was, fundamentally, an easy way for Italians to describe pizza to Americans who had never seen it before. Imagine seeing the word "pizza" or the words "tomato pie" on a menu in the early 1900s. Which item would you be more likely to try?

O'Scugnizzo Pizzeria in Utica, New York, was making its own version of the tomato pie in 1914. *Photo courtesy of O'Scugnizzo Pizzeria*

Roberto Caporuscio

Roberto Caporuscio is the owner of Don Antonio by Starita in New York City and Atlanta and Kesté Pizza and Vino in New York City. He is originally from Pontinia, Italy.

Roberto Caporuscio. *Photo courtesy of Kesté Pizza and Vino*

In your opinion, what are the traits of a great Neapolitan pizza?
A soft yet crunchy, air-filled crust with signature char marks, or "leopard" spots—and made with top-quality ingredients, beginning with the flour. The pizza cooks in ninety seconds because of the high-intensity heat from the wood-fired oven.

As the president of the Association of Neapolitan Pizza Makers (APN), in what ways have you seen pizzeria interest in the Neapolitan style grow over the years? How many American pizzerias are part of the APN?
There has been a tremendous growth in Neapolitan pizza over recent years. We see Neapolitan pizzerias popping up all over the United States. They're in remote areas, too, not just major cities. Because of media interest in Neapolitan pizza, word has spread, and people have become aware of and exposed to the pizza. Once they try it, the product speaks for itself. There are more than forty U.S. pizzerias that are part of the APN.

Those who are new to the Neapolitan style often remark that the crust is too soft and the center soupy. Can you explain why this happens?
A "soupy" pizza, with crust that is too soft, is the result of a poor-quality pizza [making process]. It happens because the pizza maker stretches the dough improperly, making it too thin.

How long does a Neapolitan-style dough need to proof compared to other styles of dough?
Neapolitan pizza dough should be proofed for a minimum of eight to nine hours. If the dough is proofed for less time, it becomes too heavy and the pizza will not be light. There are different methods of proofing, depending on the style of pizza. Neapolitan pizza dough is proofed at room temperature, while other styles are proofed in a refrigerator.

What inspired you to come to America and open a pizzeria?
I was presented with an opportunity to open a Neapolitan pizzeria in Pittsburgh. I always wanted to come to America, and this was a great way for me to learn the English language and bring Neapolitan pizza to the city.

In addition to Kesté Pizza and Vino, you now own Don Antonio by Starita, a pizzeria you opened with your mentor, Antonio Starita. What has it been like to work alongside the person who helped teach you?
To open a restaurant in New York City, the greatest city in the world, with my mentor and friend, Antonio Starita, was truly a dream come true. He is an icon in the Neapolitan pizza world and someone I've respected for many years. I'm proud to say that together we have opened our second location of Don Antonio by Starita, in Atlanta.

Tomato Pie

Recipe courtesy of Pat DePula, chef/owner of Salvatore's Tomato Pies, Sun Prairie, Wisconsin

DOUGH

4 1/2 c. unbromated, unbleached bread flour

1 3/4 tsp. kosher salt

1 tsp. instant yeast

1 3/4 c. cold water

2 tbsp. extra-virgin olive oil

Yields approx. six 6-oz. dough balls

Instructions

Pour cold water in mixing bowl of standard home mixer. Add all dry ingredients and mix on low speed until all water is absorbed. Add olive oil. Continue to mix for a total of 10 minutes or until dough is smooth. Remove from bowl and portion into whatever size balls you wish (a 16-inch pizza would require a 1 lb. 4 oz. dough ball, 10 inches requires around 9 oz.).

Roll into balls and place on a lightly floured cookie sheet. Oil the dough balls and place cookie sheet, uncovered, in fridge for 30 minutes. Then cover and let rest for at least 12 hours, but up to three days (24–48 hours is ideal). This develops flavor and texture.

A prepared dough ball that is stretched and ready for toppings is called a **SKIN**.

TOMATO PIE FOUND OUTSIDE ITS NATURAL HABITAT

Gennaro's Tomato Pie, Philadelphia, PA, gennarostomatopie.com

Nick's Tomatoe Pie, Jupiter, FL, nicks-tomatoepie.com

Salvatore's Tomato Pies, Sun Prairie, WI, salvatorestomatopies.com

Tomato Pie Pizza Joint, Los Angeles, CA, tomatopiepizzajoint.com

Tony's Pizza Napoletana, San Francisco, CA, tonyspizzanapoletana.com

SAUCE

28 oz. can high-quality crushed tomatoes

2 tsp. kosher salt

1/2 tsp. black pepper

2 tbsp. extra-virgin olive oil

Pinch of red pepper flakes

Minced or sliced garlic cloves, to taste

Whatever other herbs you'd like to add (fresh herbs taste best)

Instructions

Mix all ingredients and set aside. To allow flavors to develop, you can make the sauce ahead and place in the fridge overnight.

PIZZA PREPARATION

Coarse semolina or cornmeal, for dusting

Extra-virgin olive oil

Parmesan, freshly grated

Whole milk mozzarella

Additional toppings of your choice

Sauce you made earlier

Instructions

About 30 minutes before you're ready to make the pizzas, take the dough balls out of the fridge. Let sit at room temperature for 30 minutes. Put pizza stone on bottom of oven and set to 500–550 degrees Fahrenheit. Preheat for 40 minutes.

While waiting for oven to preheat, press out the dough, working with your hands from the center out. You may use a rolling pin if you wish, but I feel the best results are by hand.

When the pizza skin is the desired size, place on a peel dusted with coarse semolina or cornmeal so you can easily slide your pizza into the oven. Drizzle skin with extra-virgin olive oil. Dust with a good-quality, freshly grated Parmesan. Add the desired amount of whole milk mozzarella. At this point you would add your toppings of choice. Spoon your sauce on top of the cheese (do not cover the entire pizza with sauce).

Slide pizza onto pizza stone and bake for about 10 minutes or until cheese is bubbling and crust is brown.

ABOVE: Crust perfection: airy and chewy with just a bit of char.

LEFT: Mathieu Palombino, owner of Motorino in New York, experimented for months before finding his perfect dough recipe.

CRUST

Flour, water, salt, and yeast: these four simple ingredients can create a tremendously versatile palate, but they can also be some of the most difficult ingredients to work with for those striving to perfect a pizza crust. I'm sure you've noticed differences in the pizza crusts you've eaten. Some are airy while others are dense; some taste like a biscuit while others taste like bread. Minute changes in ingredient portioning and dough handling affect every pizza that comes out of the oven.

When considering the process pizza makers go through to perfect their dough formulations, I always think back to a conversation I had with Mathieu Palombino, owner of Motorino in New York, about his method for finding a dough recipe. He described how he had traveled around Naples, California, and New York, tasting pizzas before experimenting in his own kitchen. Then he equated finding his perfect dough formulation to finding the perfect pair of shoes, saying that you can search forever for a pair of shoes and then, finally, they're there! With dough, he joked that when you finally make your perfect pizza, you have to work backwards to figure out what you did to get there, from the temperature in the room to the temperature in the oven to the time you mixed the dough.

Some pizza makers are naturals, learning from a young age how to make pizza from

Every pizza maker has his or her own unique methods. Here, Al Santillo, owner of Santillo's Brick Oven Pizza in Elizabeth, New Jersey, trims away excess dough to make his pizza just right.

DOUGH PROOFING is the name of the process that occurs when dough rises.

their mothers, fathers, grandparents, etc. Other pizza makers may take months or even years to perfect a dough recipe. Jeffrey Varasano, owner of Varasano's in Atlanta, Georgia, spent nearly ten years attempting to perfect a dough recipe that would come close to that of his favorite New York pizzeria, Patsy's. His perseverance paid off, with thousands of pizza makers later turning to him for advice on how to make their own dough.

The first records of leavened bread (meaning breads containing yeast)

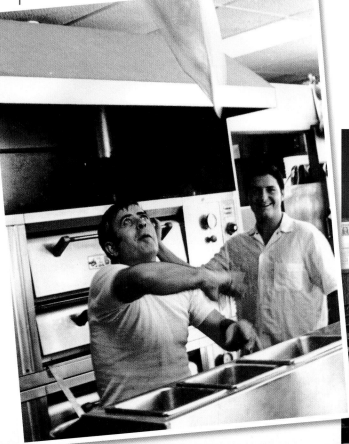

Who doesn't enjoy a good show along with their pizza? Here, Gary Amico tosses dough into the air back in the early days of DeLorenzo's in Trenton, New Jersey, and Patt Miller gives dough a spin at The Flying Pizza in Columbus, Ohio. *Amico photo courtesy of DeLorenzo's*

date back to ancient Egypt. Some say that leavened bread was discovered by Egyptians accidentally after mixing ale (which contains yeast) instead of water with flour one day. Could that be the reason pizza and beer pair so well together?

Yeast is indeed the magic ingredient that makes a pizza dough rise, or "proof." Before the Egyptians made their accidental discovery, all bread was unleavened, so early civilizations enjoyed a form of pizza on flatbreads. Yeast takes the sugar contained in flour or a sugary liquid and turns it into carbon dioxide gas and alcohol. Within dough, the bubbles produced by the yeast releasing its carbon dioxide are trapped, causing the dough to rise. In grain or fruit juice liquids, a portion of the carbon dioxide dissolves with the alcohol and produces wine and beer. Once this was discovered, beer and leavened breads using beer began showing up everywhere from the Fertile Crescent of Iran-Iraq to China and Mexico. Ancient Sumerian cuneiform tablets from 3000 BC describe bread and brew that had been transformed by fermentation.

Two strains of yeast, "high" or top yeast and "low" or bottom yeast, had been identified by the end of the eighteenth century. High yeast was

Making bread in ancient Egypt.
DEA / G. Dagli Orti / Getty Images

put on the market in 1780 by Dutch distillers specifically for bread-making, and baker's yeast was sold in cream form in 1800. By 1825, German yeast manufacturer J. H. Tebbenhoff had figured out how to extract the water and form small blocks of pure yeast; two years later, Tebbenhoff's compatriot Herr Reiminghaus discovered how to make large quantities of yeast at low cost by skimming and compressing yeast that had formed a foam surface. This process is still used today.

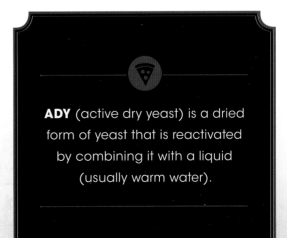

ADY (active dry yeast) is a dried form of yeast that is reactivated by combining it with a liquid (usually warm water).

While many were using yeast to ferment bread and alcohol, they didn't really understand how it worked. It wasn't until 1859 that French scientist Louis Pasteur showed the world that yeast was a living organism, forever changing culinary history.

In 1868, Charles and Max Fleischmann moved from Austria-Hungary to New York, then on to Cincinnati, Ohio, where the manufacturing industry was strong. They brought with them all the knowledge they had gained about yeast compression to a country that was still using sourdough starters. The Fleischmann brothers partnered with American businessman James Gaff to form Gaff, Fleischmann & Co. (later to become Fleischmann & Co. after Gaff's death in 1879). The yeast business grew slowly at first, but gradually success arrived, because of product reliability and ease of delivery. The company revolutionized the U.S. yeast industry—and, eventually, the U.S. pizza industry.

There are now three types of yeast (or leavening) used in bread and pizza making: instant dry yeast (dry yeast

IDY (instant dry yeast) is a form of dry yeast that can be added directly to ingredients, with no rehydration needed.

EXTRA TOPPING

What makes dough rise? Yeast is a living organism that breathes air and exhales carbon dioxide. When you give yeast air and food, it grows and produces carbon dioxide. It's this release of carbon dioxide that creates the rising dough.

Home bakers are used to making pizza with five-pound bags of flour and countertop mixers. In a pizzeria, everything is much, much bigger.

that can be added directly to dry ingredients), active dry yeast (dry yeast that reactivates in water), and sourdough starter (fermented dough saved from one recipe to use in the next).

No two dough recipes are exactly the same, and different ingredient ratios and dough additions produce different types of pizza crusts. The difference that ultimately results in different styles of pizza happens in the quantity of ingredients and how the dough is handled once it's mixed.

Flours containing higher protein create stronger dough, while flours with lower protein content produce softer dough. High-gluten flour is typically around 14 percent protein, all-purpose flour about 10 percent, and cake flour around 8 percent. This

is important to keep in mind when making different types of pizzas that may require sturdier or softer crusts.

While almost all pizza crust recipes contain essentially the same ingredients—yeast, water, flour, and salt—some add olive oil or butter to enhance the flavor of the dough. In styles such as deep-dish, higher amounts of oil (10–20 percent) impart a biscuit-like texture and taste. The more oil that's

FERMENT is another word for the process dough goes through when it rises.

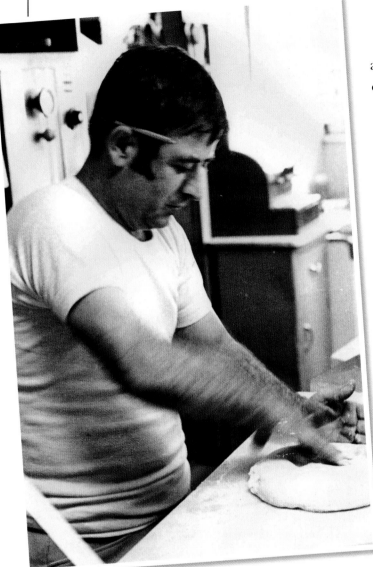

added, the more dramatic the biscuit effect is.

The amount of water in a dough recipe also has a large effect on the resulting dough. The more water added to the dough, the softer and airier the crust will be. A fairly large ratio of water (around 60 percent) is required for pizzas that will be baked in coal- and wood-fired ovens in order to allow the dough to release steam. Because of this high water content, you won't see the dough for a Neapolitan-style pizza being tossed in the air; the wet dough would simply fall apart in flight.

With so many directions to go in with pizza dough, it's a wonder there aren't more styles of pizza making a path across America today.

Pizza making is a hands-on experience, as exhibited by Gary Amico in the early years of DeLorenzo's.
Photo courtesy of DeLorenzo's

The inside cell structure of pizza is called the **CRUMB**. The best crumb is one that's airy with large holes.

A **DOUGH DOCKER** is a tool used by pizza chefs to control the amount of bubbles in the finished crust. It has tiny bumps that get rolled over the dough before baking.

- Always use a thermometer to judge water temperature for yeast. If the water is too hot, you'll kill the yeast and your dough will not rise. Try to stay around 100 degrees Fahrenheit.
- If using a pizza stone, place it in the oven before you preheat and give it plenty of time to get nice and hot. The hot surface will help mimic a deck oven.
- Mixing dough raises the temperature, so gauge your water temperature to allow for a temperature increase.
- Try to resist microwaving refrigerated pizza slices. Pop them in the oven and turn the oven to 375 degrees Fahrenheit. By the time the oven has reached temperature (around the time you start smelling the pizza), the pizza should be just about done.
- The oven temperature on the dial isn't always the true temperature. Invest in an oven thermometer to know how hot your oven is.
- Made too much pizza or brought home too many slices? Wrap them in foil and a freezer bag. They'll keep for at least a month, and you can reheat them in the oven whenever you have a craving.
- No time to knead? Ask your local pizzeria, bakery, or grocery store for ready-made dough. Just form your crust and you're ready to go.
- Has pizza given you heartburn in the past? Ditch the dried oregano and opt for a fresh variety instead.

Home-ec pizza-making, 1968. Denver Post *via Getty Images*

HOW TO MAKE IT

New York-Style Pizza Dough

Recipe courtesy of Chef Santo Bruno, corporate chef for Marsal & Sons, Inc., Lindenhurst, New York

4 c. all-purpose flour

$^1/_4$ oz. dry yeast dissolved in $^1/_4$ c. lukewarm water

1 to 1$^1/_4$ c. lukewarm water (around 60 degrees Fahrenheit)

1 tsp. salt

$^1/_4$ c. mild olive oil

Instructions

Allow dissolved yeast to double in size.

Mix all ingredients together (by hand or machine) and knead to a smooth, elastic dough.

Place in an oiled bowl and cover with a towel.

Let rest for at least 8 hours. Dough should double in size.

Divide dough into four or five balls, flattening one at a time and stretching to a thin disc about 10 inches in diameter with a thickened edge.

When ready to cook your dough, keep the toppings light (plum tomatoes crushed by hand with salt, pepper and sporadically placed mozzarella). Your pizza will cook quickly on the bottom rack of a 400-degree Fahrenheit oven.

Peter Reinhart

Peter Reinhart is the chef on assignment at Johnson & Wales University in Charlotte, North Carolina, and the author of nine books on bread and pizza.

Peter Reinhart. *Photograph by Ron Manville*

You've been on a quest to find the perfect pizza for several years, starting with your book, *American Pie*, and continuing with your blog, Pizza Quest (fornobravo.com/pizzaquest). What are some of the things you've learned about pizza during your journey?

The key is the degree of care the pizza maker (the pizzaiolo) has, coupled with sound technique and dedication to using excellent ingredients. I believe there are only two kinds of pizza: good and very good. Most pizza falls in the "good" category. My definition of "very good" is whether or not it's memorable.

You've met a lot of great pizzaiolos along the way. Who has stood out to you, and why?

Chris Bianco [Pizzeria Bianco, Phoenix] helped set the stage for artisan pizza, and that's because he personifies the dedication, passion, and craft that it takes to work at that level. Tony Gemignani [several restaurants in San Francisco, including Tony's Coal-Fired Pizza] is doing it on a broader scale. His skill and dedication to the craft is undeniable; I sometimes refer to him as the "Mozart of pizza" because he can work in so many mediums. Anthony Mangieri [Una Pizza Napoletana, San Francisco], on

the other hand, is more like the Chopin of pizza since he is more of a minimalist, working in only one style but making each pizza a personal expression of his vision. John Arena, of Metro Pizza in Vegas, is another one who can work in many styles. Nancy Silverton and her head pizzaiolo, Matt Molina, have a singular vision of their own and execute it at an amazingly high level at Pizzeria Mozza in Los Angeles. Brian Spangler in Portland, Oregon, makes a New York-style pizza and redefines how good that style can be. Jonathan Goldsmith, at Spacca Napoli in Chicago, presents the Napoletana tradition with tremendous passion. There are so many others, but these are the names that immediately come to mind. It would take me an hour to list all of the others doing great work, and there are many I haven't yet met, so I hope they will all forgive me for not listing them.

What are your tips for making great pizza crust at home?

Make the dough at least the day before, not on the same day, so that it can develop its full flavor potential. Learn to work with wetter dough than you normally would. Get your oven as hot as it will go, and bake on a baking stone or baking steel. Remember to preheat your oven *and* stone for at least forty-five minutes, so they can absorb enough heat to radiate back into the dough. Work with small pizzas at first—six to nine ounces max—until you get good at shaping. Finally, more toppings are not always better, but better-quality toppings *are* better.

Are there some basic tools you suggest using, if someone is going to bake pizza at home?

A wooden, and also a metal, pizza peel; a baking stone or steel (there is now also an aluminum pizza grate that works equally well); a scale for measuring ingredients; a metal pastry or bench blade; and a plastic bowl scraper.

ABOVE: Abate Restaurant, on Wooster Street in New Haven, Connecticut puts out some spectacular pizzas, as former President Clinton—who visited the pizzeria in 1993—can attest. *Photo courtesy* PMQ Pizza Magazine

LEFT: When you see the famous Wooster Street arch, you know you're in the pizza zone.

CHAPTER FOUR

NEW HAVEN STYLE (APIZZA) AND WHITE CLAM PIE

NEW HAVEN STYLE (APIZZA)

How to Recognize It

These pies take a trip through an oven fueled by coal or oil, with heat reaching upwards of 600 degrees Fahrenheit and pizzas baking for an extended six to eight minutes, imparting a crispy crust. The long bake time and high moisture content of New Haven-style dough results in a charred crust that may appear burnt at first sight, but that offers wonderful texture with a chewy center. Toppings are minimal—traditionally, they only include tomato and grated cheese. Pies (usually misshapen ovals in form) often arrive at the table on a wax-paper-covered square metal pan.

Where to Find It

As the name implies, you'll find this pizza, or rather "apizza" (pronounced *ah-beets* by locals) in and around New Haven, Connecticut, with the most authentic slices hailing from the pizzerias along Wooster Street. New Haven natives have spread their love for this style to other parts of the country, where some education is usually needed before people fall in love with the unique char and smoky flavor imparted by this Old-World cooking method.

I remember when I first tried New Haven-style pizza. The explosion of flavors and textures caused an uncontrollable stomping of my foot in excitement. I went to several Wooster Street pizzerias during the same trip—Sally's, Pepe's, Modern, Abate—each one delivering its own charm and nostalgia, along with some of the most memorable pizzas I've tasted over the years.

The history of New Haven-style pizza dates back to an Italian man named Frank Pepe, who began selling two simple pizzas topped with anchovies or tomatoes, grated cheese, garlic, oregano, and olive oil, from a bakery that he opened with his wife, Filomena, in 1925. They moved to the building next door in 1937 and called the restaurant Frank Pepe Pizzeria Napoletana. (The family reacquired the original location—called The Spot—in the late 1970s.)

The ovens you find in Pepe's and in America's earliest pizzerias (including those in New York, New Jersey, etc.) are usually huge—think 12 feet by 12 feet. The reason for this is that the majority of pizzeria owners were bakers before they were pizza makers, and bakeries required deep, wide

Frank Pepe and his wife, Filomena, in their first bakery, now called The Spot, located next door to Frank Pepe Pizzeria Napoletana. *Photo courtesy of Frank Pepe Pizzeria Napoletana*

ABOVE: Frank Pepe poses outside of his new pizzeria. *Photo courtesy of Frank Pepe Pizzeria Napoletana*

LEFT: The first staff at Pepe's were usually relatives. *Photo courtesy of Frank Pepe Pizzeria Napoletana*

RIGHT: Four pies ready to go into the oven at Sally's Apizza in New Haven. *Photo courtesy PMQ Pizza Magazine*

BELOW: Modern Apizza differs from Sally's and Pepe's—it is located off Wooster Street and uses an oil-fueled brick oven. However, it still cranks out some tasty New Haven-style pies. *Photo courtesy PMQ Pizza Magazine*

Two classics, tomato pie and white clam pie, at Frank Pepe Pizzeria Napoletana in New Haven. *Photo courtesy PMQ Pizza Magazine*

ovens to bake multiple loaves of bread every day.

Other New Haven pizzerias followed Pepe's lead, with Modern Apizza opening in 1934 on nearby State Street and Frank Pepe's nephew, Salvatore Consiglio, opening Sally's Apizza in 1938. There's been a longstanding rivalry—among patrons more than owners—between Sally's and Pepe's. In the same way that people argue about the differences between New York and Chicago pizza, they continually disagree over which pizza is better: Sally's or Pepe's.

It's not just coal that differentiates New Haven-style pizza from other pizzas around the nation. In fact, Modern Pizza, as well as many other area pizzerias, uses ovens powered by oil, not coal; still others use gas-fired deck ovens. Some of the characteristics that many New Haven-style pies seem to have in common are what locals call a "flat" (not thin) and tender crust, which is a result of the proofing process and the use of all-purpose flour; sauce that is never pre-cooked; the use of pecorino Romano cheese instead of mozzarella; and the use of breadcrumbs beneath the dough during baking instead of cornmeal.

Since 1938, many more New Haven-style pizzerias have opened, on Wooster Street and beyond. It's rare to find this style outside the state, but a handful of pizzerias are doing a good job of carrying on the tradition.

NEW HAVEN-STYLE PIZZA FOUND OUTSIDE ITS NATURAL HABITAT

Casanova Pizzeria, Boise, ID, casanovapizzeria.com

Coalfire, Chicago, IL, coalfirechicago.com

Double Mountain Brewery & Taproom, Hood River, OR, doublemountainbrewery.com

Max's Coal Oven Pizzeria, Atlanta, GA, maxsatl.com

Tomatoes Apizza, Farmington Hills, MI, tomatoesapizza.com

URBN, San Diego CA, urbnnorthpark.com

DIRECT DESCENDANT OF NEW HAVEN STYLE: WHITE CLAM PIE

How to Recognize It

In its purest form, the white clam pie is topped with fresh-shucked clams, olive oil, grated pecorino Romano cheese, oregano, and garlic. Most pizzerias that serve a white clam pie shuck their clams daily; a few shuck them to order. Some pizzerias use canned clams, which doesn't seem to bother clam pie fans in and around New Haven. When ordering fresh clams on your pizza, consider the climate. If you happen to visit a New Haven pizzeria and ask for a white clam pie during the winter, you may find that the pie is not available. Fresh clams can be hard to come by during the cold winter months.

Where to Find It

The white clam pie got its start at Frank Pepe Pizzeria Napoletana. Pepe had been serving raw littleneck clams from Rhode Island on the half shell as an appetizer; these found their way onto the pizzas sometime around the 1950s. The popularity of the pie grew as the years passed, and now you can find white clam pies at nearly every pizzeria in New Haven. The major distinction seems to be between the use of fresh and canned clams, both of which have their own fans.

ABOVE: Pizzerias outside of New Haven that offer coal-fired pizza often place coal directly inside the oven (instead of using a connected oven chamber), as seen here at Max's Coal Oven Pizzeria in Atlanta.

LEFT: Coalfire in Chicago stands out from surrounding deep-dish and thin-crust Chicago institutions with its New Haven-style pies.

HOW TO MAKE IT

Clams Casino Napolitano

Recipe courtesy of Lou Abate, owner, Abate Apizza, Wooster Street, New Haven

Cornmeal (enough to lightly dust pizza peel)

17 oz. pizza dough ball (Neapolitan style or New York style will work best)

Extra virgin olive oil (enough for oiling skin and brushing crust)

10 oz. whole milk mozzarella, shredded

1 fresh suntan bell pepper, thinly sliced (bell peppers will also work)

10 oz. fresh cherrystone clams, roughly chopped

Butcher-ground or coarse black pepper, to taste

3 cloves of fresh garlic, chopped

20 bacon slices

2 oz. imported pecorino Romano cheese, ground

Pinch of oregano

Instructions

Stretch dough ball to 16 inches diameter and place on pizza peel that has been lightly dusted with cornmeal. Oil pizza skin with extra virgin olive oil and apply whole milk mozzarella and suntan peppers. Add fresh cherrystone clams and lightly sprinkle with pepper. Add garlic and cover entire pie with bacon slices. Gently cover pizza with pecorino Romano cheese. Sprinkle a pinch of oregano and brush crust with extra virgin olive oil. Bake at 550 degrees Fahrenheit, until crust is dark brown.

TOMATO PIES MADE TO ORDER

GRATED CHEESE
MOZZARELLA
ANCHOVIES
ONION
PEPPERS
CHICKEN
FRESH CLAMS
SHRIMP

PEPPERONI
BACON
SALAMI
SAUSAGE
MUSHROOM
BROCCOLI
SPINACH

COMBINATION PIES PRICED ACCORDINGLY

BEER   SODA   COFFEE
ICED TEA   WINE

NOT RESPONSIBLE FOR PERSONAL PROPERTY

ABOVE: A thing of beauty: the Sicilian from Di Fara in Brooklyn, New York.

LEFT: A nice, well-done bottom, with spots of char, is the sign of a perfectly cooked crust.

CHAPTER FIVE

SICILIAN PIZZA AND GRANDMA PIZZA

SICILIAN PIZZA

How to Recognize It

Most easily recognized by its placement of sauce above the cheese and a thick one- to two-inch crust, Sicilian pizza is rectangular in shape with a thick, crunchy base and an airy interior. Toppings are minimal with this style, which is typically found with just cheese and sauce.

Where to Find It

Sicilian pizza, and versions of it, can be found across the country, with heavy concentrations in the Northeast. When I first tried it on a trip to New York, it immediately reminded me of the Detroit-style pizza I grew up with in Michigan. Detroit style also uses seasoned pans (albeit of a slightly different shape) and the same topping order (sauce on top). There's clearly a connection there. Round "pan" pizzas, which use a deep pan to help crisp the oiled dough, are also reminiscent of the Sicilian style.

What we call Sicilian pizza in America is actually called *sfincione* in Sicily. There, the sfincione is square bread that's sold in local bakeries and topped with a sauce of tomatoes, onions, anchovies, and breadcrumbs. In lieu of mozzarella, bakers dust a hard cheese over the top.

When sfincione was first being sold in the States, it stayed fairly true to form, as it was topped simply with tomato sauce and a dusting of cheese. As years passed, however, more pizzerias started adding mozzarella to the recipe in order to appease American tastes. Now it's rare to find a true slice of sfincione. Most have been transformed into what we call Sicilian, featuring a layer of mozzarella under the sauce.

Some of the best Sicilian I've had has been in Brooklyn, at J&V Pizzeria in Bensonhurst and L&B Spumoni Gardens, near Coney Island. Surprisingly, another great square was found at a place called The Flying Pizza near Ohio State University in Columbus, Ohio, a few years back.

Part of what helps give Sicilian pies their signature flavor and crunch are the steel pans they're baked in.

With Sicilian pies, the focus is sometimes on the sauce—like on this one from L&B Spumoni Gardens in Brooklyn, New York—and sometimes on the cheese, such as on the pie at Original Presto's in West New York, New Jersey (RIGHT). Either way you go, you still get the thick, chewy crust with a crispy, buttery base.

SICILIAN-STYLE PIZZA FOUND OUTSIDE ITS NATURAL HABITAT

Big Mario's New York Style Pizza, Seattle, WA, bigmariosnewyorkstylepizza.com

Pinocchio's Pizza & Subs, Cambridge, MA, pinocchiospizza.net

Sicilian Thing Pizza, San Diego, CA, sicilianthingpizza.com

The Flying Pizza, Columbus, OH, theflyingpizza.com

Zoli's NY Pizza, Dallas, TX, zolispizza.com

SICILIAN'S SECOND COUSIN: GRANDMA PIZZA

How to Recognize It

A grandma pizza is, for all intents and purposes, a thinner version of a Sicilian pizza. The thickness of the pizza falls somewhere between New York style and Sicilian. All the other attributes lean toward Sicilian, except that grandma pizzas may be slightly crispier than Sicilians, since they're thinner.

Where to Find It

Grandma pizzas are not as common as Sicilian pizzas, but their numbers have been growing in recent years. You'll most often find a grandma in the same place where you'll find a Sicilian (but it's not a guarantee).

J&V Pizzeria in Brooklyn, New York, has been serving up grandma slices for decades.

Who can say no to grandma? Check out this grandma slice from La Villa Pizzeria in Brooklyn.

Widely accepted as first being introduced by Umberto's Pizzeria in New Hyde Park, New York, the credit for grandma pizza goes to the owner's mother, who used to make the pizza in Italy using the same ingredients as those of a Sicilian pie (tomatoes, anchovies, no cheese). Umberto's Americanized the pie by adding mozzarella and began selling it to customers in the late 1980s. The style started getting more notice around the year 2000.

Just as an Italian grandma would make it at home, the assembly of a grandma pie is an easy one. It consists of pressing dough into a square pan that's coated with olive oil, placing

EXTRA TOPPING

The first American cookbook recipe for pizza appeared in *Specialita Culinarie Italiane, 137 Tested Recipes of Famous Italian Foods*, a fundraising cookbook published in Boston in 1936. The recipe was for a Neapolitan pie, or *Pizza alla Napolitana*.

"The first pizza that you experience as a child becomes the pizza of your dreams and the pizza by which you judge all other pizza."

—*Food critic Ed Levine*

mozzarella on top of the dough, and topping it all with random spots of sauce made from drained and hand-crushed plum tomatoes, garlic, oregano, olive oil, basil, and salt. Additional olive oil drizzled atop and under the pie before it bakes ensures a crispy bottom and singe-free top.

Many believe that the grandma pie is what the original Sicilian-style pizza looked like in Italy, before it was brought over to America, and that it gradually evolved into the thicker Sicilian-style pie we're now used to. What's more likely is that the pizza's thickness depended on the person making the pizza, since in the beginning, these were mainly home-baked pies in Italy and America.

HOW TO MAKE IT

Grandma Pie

Try this recipe from Jay Jerrier, owner of Zoli's NY Pizza in Dallas.

DOUGH

2 tbsp. plus 1 tsp. Sicilian sea salt

1/2 tsp. sugar

1/4 tsp. fresh cake yeast

3 1/2 c. tap water with 1 small handful of ice

2 tbsp. extra-virgin olive oil, plus more for oiling the dough and pan

7 c. bread flour

Instructions

Combine salt, sugar, and yeast and slowly mix in olive oil.

Add water and mix for 3 minutes on medium speed.

Add flour and mix for 5 minutes on medium high until dough pulls away from side of mixing bowl.

Remove dough from mixer and cover with wet towels. Let rest 1 hour at room temperature.

Section dough into 24 oz. dough balls (should get two dough balls) and place on oiled cooking sheet covered in plastic wrap. Make sure to oil the top of the dough balls so the plastic doesn't stick.

Let rest in refrigerator for 18–24 hours.

The next day, remove dough from fridge, and let come to room temperature. Using a 16x16x1 "Sicilian" pizza pan (dark "blue steel" available online), oil the bottom and sides generously with extra-virgin olive oil. Stretch the dough ball into the pan, trying to reach the sides—it's okay if it doesn't go all the way to the corners. It will relax as it proofs.

Cover with plastic and let proof in a warm area of your kitchen for 1–2 hours.

The dough should begin to spread to the corners.

Preheat oven to 550 degrees Fahrenheit.

SAUCE

1 28 oz. can Italian plum tomatoes (San Marzano style)

1 28 oz. can California plum tomatoes

1 clove garlic, minced

1 good-sized pinch dried oregano

4 basil leaves, chopped

2 tbsp. extra-virgin olive oil

1 tbsp. salt

Instructions

Combine all tomatoes in a bowl and crush each tomato individually by hand (do not blend tomatoes with a machine).

Add remaining ingredients and mix to a chunky consistency.

Preparation

Take the dough you've proofed in the pan and pull the corners to the edges of the pan.

Cover it to the edges with your favorite shredded mozzarella (you should use about 10–12 oz. of mozzarella). You can also mix in a bit of provolone if you'd like.

Scatter some grated Parmigiano Reggiano across the pizza, making sure to cover all of the edges and corners.

Using a big spoon, drop "dollops" of your chunky tomato sauce across the crust (don't cover the entire crust with sauce). Take care not to deflate the proofed crust when adding cheese and sauce.

Place the pizza onto the middle rack of a 550-degree Fahrenheit oven.

Bake 5–7 minutes.

Rotate the pizza 180 degrees, and bake an additional 5 minutes or until cheese is bubbly and browned on top.

Check the bottom of the pizza. It should be golden brown and crispy—almost fried in the oil from the bottom of the pan.

Cut the pizza into 9 slices. Don't worry if the bottom is not crispy. You can reheat slices on a pizza stone, skillet, or cookie sheet and they will crisp right up.

If you look around, you can sometimes find Sicilian slices outside of their region, such as at The Flying Pizza in Columbus, Ohio.

Adam Kuban

Adam Kuban is the New York City-based founder of Slice, the pizza blog for Serious Eats (slice.seriouseats.com).

Adam Kuban. *Photograph by Robyn Lee*

We all love pizza, but what inspired you to make a career out of writing about it?

I fell into it, really. When I first moved to New York City in 2000, I assumed someone would have a "fan website" about pizza—something that documented the best pizzerias in NYC. There was nothing online at the time, so when simple blogging platforms sprang up in 2003, I had the perfect outlet to create my own guide to NYC pizza, which became Slice. I just made it up as I went along, inviting the audience to join me, weigh in, and direct the exploration, too. It was a

hobby at first, and then in 2006 SeriousEats.com bought Slice from me and hired me on full-time as the founding editor, where I continued to write for it and edit it.

You've visited a lot of pizzerias over the years. Which ones have been the most memorable, and why?

I love the old-school places with a story, a family that's been at it for generations, tables or booths that have a time-worn patina to them and pizza that lives up to all those attributes. Totonno's in Brooklyn, Patsy's in East Harlem, Maria's Pizza in Milwaukee, Sally's Apizza in New Haven. Those places speak to me like no other, partially because I dream of opening a pizzeria of my own, and I aspire to that same kind of longevity and intergenerational customer loyalty.

In your opinion, what is it about pizza that draws us all to it again and again?

There's just unending variation to pizza. Get tired of plain cheese? Add some toppings. Get tired of those toppings? Switch it up. Get tired of that? Switch pizza styles altogether and run through the toppings gamut again. Within each genre of pizza there are dozens and sometimes hundreds of pizzerias to explore. It never gets old. And of course, one of the best things about pizza is that you almost *have* to share it. So even a lackluster pizza can make for a great pizza *experience*, if you have the right company.

In your opinion, what makes for a truly great pizza?

For me, crust is king. Whether it's a Neapolitan-, New York-, New Haven-, or bar-style pizza. The crust has to have flavor, yet at the same time not overwhelm the toppings. If the crust is bad, the pizza can't be called good.

How can novices or those visiting a new city train themselves to pick out a great pizzeria before walking through the door?

Hah! You think it's that easy? Well, honestly, as a guy who made his mark in the pizza world via the web, I'm going to have to go with "the Internet." Do some research. Check out the various pizza websites out there. In addition to Slice, pizzamaking.com, and IDreamofPizza. com, many other regional pizza blogs and sites have sprung up in the last decade. I also like to use the Foursquare app to find good pizza, and even Yelp to get a lay of the land. They're not always going to jibe with any one individual's preference, but they'll give you an idea of what people think is popular. Also, I like to take to Twitter and Facebook and ask my network of friends. Chances are, someone in your social circles will have a good suggestion.

Do you make pizza at home? What are your pizzeria aspirations?

Yes. I make pizza at home at least twice a week. I'm doing an apprenticeship/training at Paulie Gee's in Brooklyn, where I do one pizza making shift a week (and until recently had been doing a prep shift on Sundays. too). The plan is that I'll be opening the Portland branch of Paulie Gee's as Paul Giannone expands to other cities. So, yes, I do aspire to open my own joint. As far as homemade pizza goes, I've been chasing down a great bar pie recipe for almost a year now. I'm hoping to do a bar-pie pop-up night in NYC before I move to Portland to open Paulie Gee's PDX.

REGULAR PIZZA $7.95
PIZZA WITH EXTRA CHEESE $8.95
PIZZA WITH EXTRA CHEESE, PLUS
    MORE CHEESE STUFFED INTO CRUST ... $9.95
PIZZA WITH EXTRA CHEESE, PLUS
    CHEESE STUFFED INTO CRUST
    ATOP A BED OF CHEESE $10.95
JUST A TON OF CHEESE –
    NO QUESTIONS ASKED $11.95

R. Chast

ABOVE: © Roz Chast / *The New Yorker* Collection / The Cartoon Bank
LEFT: Fontina Val d'Aosta (made from cow's milk in the Aosta Valley of Italy) is the shining star of this mixed mushroom pizza from Milo & Olive in Santa Monica, California.

CHAPTER SIX

CHEESE

What's pizza without cheese, right? Whether it's a sprinkling of Romano on a tomato pie, slices of creamy mozzarella di bufala on a Neapolitan-style pizza, or gooey, part-skim shredded mozzarella on a New York-style slice, pizza simply tastes better with cheese.

You may shudder to imagine a time when pizza was void of cheese, but in ancient times, flatbreads and focaccias were topped solely with simple herbs, vegetables, and anything else accessible at the time. According to the International Dairy Foods Association, travelers from Asia may have brought cheese-making to Europe. During the Middle Ages, monks in European monasteries began making and improving cheese. Italy was to become the cheese-making capital of Europe during the tenth century.

When the Pilgrims brought cheese with them to the New World in 1620, farmers started producing it in small quantities—until 1851, when Jesse Williams opened the first cheese factory in Oneida County, New York. By 1880, there were 3,923 dairy factories nationwide, and by 1920, 418 million pounds of cheese were being produced by factories each year.

Mark Todd, a.k.a. "The Cheese Dude," is a culinary consultant at the California Milk Advisory Board. He explains that different cheeses provide different stretch, coverage, and browning, while also helping to build a unique

The white pizza at Coalfire in Chicago features mozzarella, ricotta, and Romano.

LEFT: Tableside mozzarella. If you ever see this on a menu, get it. You will never forget the taste of just-made mozzarella.
BELOW: Prepping the mozzarella for the day at Pizza Fusion, a pizza chain focused on natural and organic menu items.

flavor profile. He says that typical blends always start with at least 80 percent mozzarella.

You'll find that most pizzerias use mozzarella in some form or another (mozzarella di bufala, fior di latte, *burrata,* whole-milk, part-skim, smoked), while many blend another cheese in (provolone, Parmesan, and cheddar are the most common) or grate a cheese on top when the pie exits the oven (usually Parmesan or pecorino Romano).

Personally, I love a fresh mozzarella on Neapolitan-style pies, but I'm just as content with a part-skim mozzarella blend on anything from a New York- to California-style pizza. And once you start adding toppings, the cheese can go in a whole different direction. There are proteins and vegetables that are immediately enhanced by certain cheeses, and part of the fun of exploring pizza is sampling those differences.

MOZZARELLA CRASH COURSE:

Mozzarella di Bufala–Made from the milk of domesticated water buffalo in Italy, this cheese can be found on Neapolitan-style pizzas. Today it appears in many more pizzerias than it has in the past, as more places now have easy access to imported goods from Italy. This is a high-moisture mozzarella that is perishable within a matter of days, unless purchased in a vacuum-sealed container.

Fior di latte–Also highly perishable, this mozzarella is similar to mozzarella di bufala but is made from cow's milk instead of water buffalo. The taste is slightly less milky and the consistency is not quite as creamy as mozzarella di bufala, but it will definitely do in a pinch.

Burrata–This fresh Italian cheese has become popular in America just over the past five years or so. It features an outer shell of mozzarella and an inner filling of mozzarella and cream. Its buttery texture takes mozzarella to a whole new level, and it is best when served at the peak of freshness.

Whole-Milk and Part-Skim Mozzarella (pizza cheese)–You'll find these cheeses being used in the majority of pizzerias across the United States. They have a long shelf life and provide that signature stretch we've all become so accustomed to seeing.

ABOVE: Olio in Los Angeles replaces traditional mozzarella with burrata on its Margherita pie.
BELOW: Fresh burrata topped with olive oil and basil.

(Those with lactose intolerance may be surprised to find that pizza is not off-limits. Cheese is actually much less threatening to a lactose-intolerant person than other dairy products, such as milk. With a little experimentation, many can still enjoy cheeses that contain low levels of lactose, such as Parmesan, Swiss, aged cheddar, and other firm or semi-firm cheeses that have been drained of their whey/lactose.)

Cheese has become synonymous with pizza in America, and the doubling of American cheese consumption over the past thirty years proves how much we love the stuff. Thankfully, there's no shortage when it comes to cheese variety, and pizzerias will continue to introduce new blends every day to satisfy our cravings. Some of our favorite cheeses to enjoy on pizza in America, besides traditional mozzarella, include cheddar, Parmesan, Monterey Jack, Asiago, blue, Gruyère, Romano, gorgonzola, feta, and Tallegio. It's true that most of these cheeses originated outside of America, but they all taste great on any Americanized style of pizza.

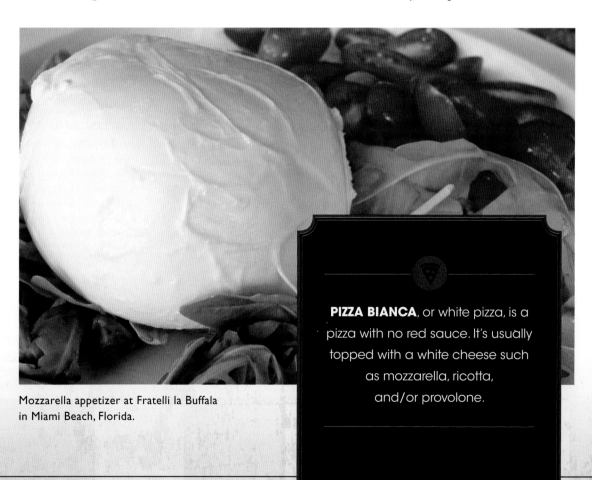

Mozzarella appetizer at Fratelli la Buffala in Miami Beach, Florida.

PIZZA BIANCA, or white pizza, is a pizza with no red sauce. It's usually topped with a white cheese such as mozzarella, ricotta, and/or provolone.

TOPS IN TOPPINGS

Man can't live on cheese alone, so let's take a look at some of America's favorite pizza toppings.

ANCHOVIES–These small saltwater fish related to herring have been enjoyed by the Greeks and Romans for centuries. Not many anchovy pizzas are ordered in America, by comparison. The traditional Italian fashion involves eating them with just marinara sauce and no cheese. Many pizzerias carry them for purely nostalgic reasons.

© Tom Cheney / *The New Yorker* Collection / The Cartoon Bank

DIPPING SAUCES–The habit of dipping pizza crust in sauce most likely began innocently, with someone asking for a side of marinara sauce to dip their extra pizza crust. We've gradually grown to think of almost every sauce as one that can be used as a crust enhancer. The Whitewater, Wisconsin-based Toppers Pizza menu offers pizza sauce, nacho cheese, ranch, garlic butter, smoky BBQ, salsa, sour cream, blue cheese, hot buffalo, mild buffalo, bacon honey mustard, parmesan garlic, and sweet chili.

HAM AND PINEAPPLE–Most New York pizzerias will laugh you out the door if you try to order this combo, more commonly known as a Hawaiian pizza. Introduced by Greek restaurateur Sam Panopoulos in 1962—at his Chinese restaurant in Chatham, Ontario—the pizza was an instant hit, despite the fact that its inventor had never seen a pizza before.

OLIVE OIL–In addition to being an occasional dough and sauce additive, extra-virgin olive oil also serves as a great flavor enhancer and scorch barrier when applied just prior to a pizza's entry into the oven. Extra-virgin olive oil is high in healthy monounsaturated fats, which can help to lower cholesterol and control insulin levels. When purchasing olive oil for yourself, choose oils that are

(continued on page 80)

(continued from page 79)

At a pizzeria, you never want to run out of olive oil.

packaged in dark containers. (These help block light, which can cause oxidation.) Store your oil in a room-temperature cupboard for up to a year.

PEPPERONI–Consistently ranked as America's favorite pizza topping, this spicy, air-cured, smoked sausage does not exist in Italy, where you'll find mostly salami. Pepperoni was introduced to the culinary world in the early 1900s and is an Italian-American gift to pizza. In Italy, asking for a "pepperoni" pizza will get you a pizza topped with green peppers.

ONIONS AND OLIVES–These ingredients were widely used in Italy for topping focaccias and pizzas, so it wasn't uncommon to see them when pizza arrived in the United States. Onions were found on early pies and in marinara sauces. They're still one of our favorite toppings. Olives have also been used for centuries, with some pizzerias offering green olives in addition to the black variety. The canned black olives you find on pizza are actually green olives that have been cured to turn black.

OREGANO–Originally used as a replacement for basil since it's also from the mint family, oregano is widely referred to as the "pizza herb." It can be found in tomato sauces and sprinkled on the tops of pizzas everywhere. While you'll find dried oregano more often than fresh in a pizzeria setting, dried oregano is often the culprit behind the heartburn some associate with pizza. If you regularly experience heartburn when you order pizza out, ask if it's possible to get your pie without oregano.

MEATS–Pizza stuck to tomatoes and vegetables for the most part until around 1920, when meat-packing towns such as Chicago started topping their pizzas with meat. This was a big hit at the bars that were serving pizzas to hungry patrons, and at the pizzerias that fed hungry workers during the industrial age. Sausage is still one of the top sellers in Chicago.

MUSHROOMS–Enjoyed on flatbreads and pizzas since prehistoric times, mushrooms are one of the most popular pizza toppings. Depending on each individual pizzeria's offerings, you will find canned or fresh mushrooms on your pizza. Fresh ones are often sautéed before they are added to pizza, to eliminate some of the moisture they release and to impart a bit more flavor.

EXTRA TOPPING

Canned black olives are actually ripe green olives that have been soaked in a solution and allowed to oxidize and turn black.

ABOVE: A protective wall of crust holds all of the cheese and vegetables in this stuffed pizza at Chicago-based Giordano's.

LEFT: In addition to a hefty dose of ingredients on the inside, deep-dish pizza also features a buttery, biscuit-like crust and hearty tomato sauce on top.

CHAPTER SEVEN

DEEP-DISH PIZZA

DEEP-DISH PIZZA

How to Recognize It

This is easily the most recognizable of all the pizza styles. A deep-dish pizza is anywhere from one to three inches thick, with a deep crust that holds a variety of layered ingredients, in reverse order—cheese is first, then meats (sometimes a large patty of sausage in the shape of the crust), vegetables, and a final topping of crushed tomatoes. Pan pizzas are sometimes mislabeled as deep-dish in some parts of the country, but a true deep-dish pizza has a thin to medium crust that only appears thick because it's holding so many ingredients.

Where to Find It

It's possible to find deep-dish pizza in several regions of the country, due to the franchising of pizza companies and the relocation of individual pizzeria owners, but the highest concentration of deep-dish pizza is in Chicago.

It took a bit of experimentation, but over the years, I've gradually learned the best way to eat a deep-dish pizza to suit my tastes. My first time out, I tried a cheese deep-dish and was overwhelmed by the amount of cheese. During subsequent attempts, I tried meats and/or veggies with my cheese.

My favorite has to be the veggie-lover deep-dish. You still get all of the cheese and sauce with that biscuit-like crust, but the vegetables help to break up the weight of the pie. A couple of my favorites are at Pequod's Pizza and Giordano's—both in Chicago.

Many say that the advent of deep-dish pizza was the first time pizza really became Americanized. When Pizzeria Uno opened in 1943, those who were already eating pizza in Chicago were eating crust so thin that it was regularly compared to a cracker. (Thin crust is still a very popular style in Chicago, but the deep-dish pie is what most tourists think of when they think of Chicago.)

So why did Ike Sewell, along with restaurateur Ric Riccardo, decide to throw a pizza curveball with Pizzeria Uno, introducing gut-busting pizzas that looked more like casseroles than the pizzas people were growing accustomed to? It may have had something to do with the fact that Sewell was from Texas, where the "Everything's bigger in Texas" motto rings true. Another lesser-known theory has to do with Sewell's thirty-two-year-long career (from 1933 until 1965) as a liquor salesman. The additional time it took a deep-dish pie to cook allowed patrons plenty of leisure time to drink a couple bottles of wine.

LEFT: The deep-dish at Pequod's Pizza in Chicago is a bit thinner and showcases some caramelization around the edges, proving that not all deep-dish pizza is created equal.
OPPOSITE PAGE, INSET: Jean, Marc, Rick, and Lou Malnati on opening day of Lou Malnati's Pizzeria in 1971. *Photo courtesy of Lou Malnati's*

EXTRA TOPPING

The largest round pizza ever made, according to the World Record Academy, was the creation of Dovilio Nardi and four other Italian chefs. The 2012 pizza was 131 feet in diameter and weighed 51,257 pounds. (It was also gluten-free.)

Lou Malnati (standing) serves a pie to his father, Rudy, in the early days of Pizzeria Uno, before Lou left to open Lou Malnati's Pizzeria. *Photo courtesy of Lou Malnati's*

ABOVE: No one leaves hungry when a deep-dish pizza hits the table. *Photo courtesy of Lou Malnati's*

While there are disagreements over the true origins of deep-dish pizza, the most widely accepted story has it that Sewell came to Chicago from Texas looking to open a Mexican food restaurant. He asked Riccardo to help him in the venture, but Riccardo was Italian and had never cooked Mexican food before. After trying Mexican food and becoming ill, Riccardo retreated to Italy. He returned with a new idea for a pizza restaurant. Following much experimentation in the kitchen, Sewell and Riccardo came up with what we know today as deep-dish pizza.

Not surprisingly, the pizza didn't take off right away. According to a *Chicago Tribune* interview with Sewell in 1987, people didn't recognize deep-dish as pizza, and Uno had to give away strips of it at the bar. They refinanced the restaurant three times during the first year and were on the brink of shutting down. Things didn't turn around until a reporter came in and wrote a rave review about the restaurant. A second outpost, Pizzeria Due, was established in 1955 to accommodate the increasing number of customers. (The St. Lawrence Seaway, a project that began in the 1940s and was completed in 1959, may have helped to bring in customers in the early years. The canal system

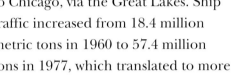
allowed ships to travel from Canada to Chicago, via the Great Lakes. Ship traffic increased from 18.4 million metric tons in 1960 to 57.4 million tons in 1977, which translated to more workers and more visitors.)

As with most stories in pizza's history, the deep-dish family tree branched off from its roots. Some of Pizzeria Uno's original partners and employees went on to open their own historic pizzerias featuring the popular deep-dish pie, such as Gino's East in 1966 and Lou Malnati's in 1971.

Deep-dish pizza takes a special set of skills, and tools, to perfect. It's prepared in specially made round steel pans that can accommodate the hefty pies. The pans get oiled prior to baking so that the pizzas don't stick, and you get a nice "fried" effect when the pizza is done baking. Most deep-dish pizzas, unless partially baked before the toppings go on, or unless cooked in a special oven, require extended cooking times of up to forty-five minutes.

The addition of oil in the dough and pan helps to provide a nice crunch and allows the crust to hold up under the mass of toppings. For years, many have assumed cornstarch and/or semolina flour were what gave deep-dish pizza its signature color and crunch, but this has since been proven to be a long-standing Chicago myth.

Pizzerias in other parts of the country enjoy trying out the deep-dish style. This potato and egg deep-dish pie was a brunch special promotion at Fritti, a Neapolitan-style pizzeria in Atlanta.

Chicago-Style Pizza Dough

Recipe courtesy of Tom "The Dough Doctor" Lehmann

(Note: This recipe provides baker's percentages and standard measurements.)

Water: 57%—1 cup (8 oz./227 grams)

Active dry yeast: 0.75%—(0.1 oz./3 grams)

Flour: 100%—3 cups (about 14 ounces)

Salt: 1.75%—1½ tsp. (0.25 oz./7 grams)

Sugar: 2%—1¾ tsp. (0.28 oz./8 grams)

Butter, melted: 2%—½ tbsp. (0.25 oz./7 grams)

Olive oil: 2%—½ tbsp. (0.25 oz./7 grams)

BAKER'S PERCENTAGES is a weight-based measuring system used by bakers in which every ingredient is listed in relation to the 100 percent weight of flour.

Instructions

Adjust the water temperature to give a finished (mixed) dough temperature of 80 to 85 degrees Fahrenheit. As a general rule, this will necessitate using water at about 80 degrees Fahrenheit.

Add the water to the mixing bowl and suspend the yeast in the water.

Add the flour and then the rest of the dry ingredients.

Melt the butter into the olive oil and slowly add it to the dough while mixing at low speed for 30 seconds.

Mix the dough until only about ¾ of the flour is hydrated. DO NOT mix until all of the flour is wet.

Transfer the partially mixed dough to a suitably sized container, cover to prevent drying, and allow the dough to ferment for 4 to 6 hours at room temperature.

Cut the dough into desired weight pieces and manually form into loose "pucks."

Put the dough pucks into dough boxes or into plastic bags and refrigerate overnight.

On the following day, remove dough from the cooler and allow warming at room temperature for 1½ to 2 hours, then sheet the dough to the desired thickness. For thin crusts start with 3/16-inch thickness, and for thick crusts start with 3/8-inch thickness. Adjust the dough thickness to give the desired crust thickness.

Cut the sheeted dough to desired diameter. Thin crusts should be docked, topped, and taken directly to the oven for baking. Thick crusts do not need to be docked. Place the dough into a dark-colored, deep-dish pan, which has been greased with table-grade margarine or clarified butter.

Thin-crust pizzas are best baked directly on the hearth, but you can also bake them on a screen or disk if you have an impingement oven. Thick crusts need to be allowed to proof for 45 to 70 minutes before topping and baking.

With thick-crust pizzas, put the cheese on first (slices work best), followed by the sauce, and then add the toppings and maybe just a light sprinkling of cheese. (Parmesan is my personal favorite.)

ABOVE: The three signs of a Detroit-style pizza: thick crust, caramelized edges, and random sauce placement.
Photo courtesy of Detroit Style Pizza Company

LEFT: Detroit-style pizza for the meat lover.
Photo courtesy of Detroit Style Pizza Company

DETROIT STYLE

DETROIT STYLE

How to Recognize It

A close relative of Sicilian pizza, Detroit-style pizza stands out with its airy interior; thick, crunchy crust; and toppings that go all the way across, creating caramelized cheese along the edges. Toppings are reversed here, with traditional toppings, including pepperoni, followed by cheese, with just a drizzling of sauce on top.

Where to Find It

Until recently, Detroit-style pizza was pretty much confined to Michigan, and really to the Detroit area in general. However, as people move away from Detroit, we see it as far away as Austin, Telluride, and Las Vegas. One enterprising pizzeria operator, Shawn Randazzo, who worked in the second pizzeria run by the founding father of Detroit-style pizza (Cloverleaf Bar & Restaurant), is currently on a mission to spread the Detroit-style pizza gospel to even more parts of the country with his Detroit Style Pizza Co., founded in 2012.

Gus Guerra, who had owned the Detroit-based bar Buddy's Rendezvous since 1936, decided in 1946 that he wanted to start offering food to his customers in an effort to increase profits. Not wanting to follow other area restaurants that were adding fish and chips, he turned to his mother-in-law from Sicily for ideas. She showed him how to make the square pie with reverse toppings still being made today by the Guerra family and many others.

Guerra sold Buddy's in 1953 after a business dispute and struck out on his own. He opened Cloverleaf, which is still run by members of the Guerra family, in Eastpointe, Michigan. Additional pizzerias that spawned from the original Buddy's include Sorrento in Warren and Loui's Pizza in Hazel Park.

Detroit-style pizza is baked in thick, rectangular, blue steel pans that were never really designed for baking, but rather to hold small parts in factories. (Detroit was the center of the automobile industry, after all.) The unique pans act similarly to a cast-iron skillet in the way they retain and impart flavor to the pizzas. Almost every pizzeria that makes Detroit-style pizza orders its pans from the same manufacturer in West Virginia, which can sometimes result in a pan shortage.

The history behind the now-famous pizza pans can be traced back to an old Detroit legend, according to which a friend of Guerra's who worked in a factory gave him his first batch of pans. It's the pans that make Detroit-style pizza truly unique. Without them, the pies would be Sicilian. The pans set the

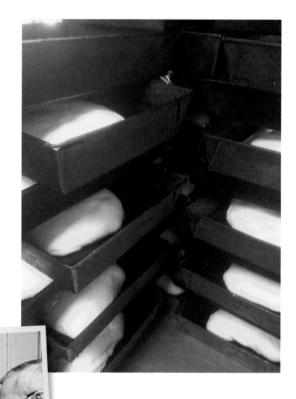

ABOVE: Part of what delivers that Detroit-style crunch are the blue steel pans used to bake the pies, originally manufactured to hold small factory parts. *Photo courtesy of Detroit Style Pizza Company*

LEFT: Friends playing cards over pizza and beers at Buddy's Rendezvous in Detroit. *Photo courtesy of Buddy's Rendezvous*

LEFT: Detroit-style pizza began with Gus Guerra in 1946. Here he enjoys a slice at his Cloverleaf Bar in Eastpointe, Michigan. *Photo courtesy of Cloverleaf Bar & Restaurant*

BELOW: Some of the first crew members at Buddy's Rendezvous, making pizza and salads. *Photo courtesy of Buddy's Rendezvous*

Detroit style apart from others because they assist in the caramelization of the cheese, which is deliberately pushed up the sides of the extra-deep pans. To ensure an extra crisp crust, pies are usually removed from the pan when they are almost done baking, then placed directly on the deck of the oven.

Traditional toppings include pepperoni and a blend of mozzarella and Brick cheese (a semi-hard cow's milk cheese from Wisconsin with a taste similar to sharp cheddar cheese, which derives its name from the original process of using bricks to press moisture out of the cheese). These are added before the pizza enters the oven. Warm spoons of marinara are added when the pie makes its exit.

The tool used to maneuver pizzas in and out of the oven is called a **PEEL**. It is most often made of wood or aluminum.

Breaking for pizza. Buddy's Rendezvous waitress Connie and manager Irv sit down to enjoy some wine and pizza. *Photo courtesy of Buddy's Rendezvous*

Some pizzerias serving Detroit-style pizza bake the pizza twice to ensure a crispier crust and picture-perfect caramelization around all sides.

Why top the pizza in reverse order? For the same reasons as the Sicilian pie: when tomato sauce is applied last, the toppings and dough can cook more evenly, eliminating the chances of a soggy crust.

DETROIT-STYLE PIZZA FOUND OUTSIDE ITS NATURAL HABITAT

Brown Dog Pizza, Telluride, CO, browndogpizza.com

Klausie's Pizza, Raleigh, NC, klausies.com

Norm's Wayside, Buffalo, MN, normswayside.com

Northside Nathan's, Las Vegas, NV, northsidenathanslasvegas.com

Via 313, Austin, TX, via313.com

JESSE RYAN

Jesse Ryan, of Chatsworth, Georgia, is the #1 Mellow Mushroom Super Fan. Mellow Mushroom Pizza, inventors of the Classic Southern Pizza, was founded in Atlanta in 1974. Today it has over one hundred fifty locations.

Jesse Ryan. *Courtesy Jesse Ryan*

How did you get the title of "#1 Mellow Mushroom Super Fan"? Is that an official title?
At a Mellow Mushroom opening, I had the pleasure of meeting one of the founders. I told him I was his company's number one fan, that I had been to almost fifty locations, had studied everything about his company, and felt that I knew way more about Mellow Mushroom than the average fan. It was at that moment that someone from the art department said I was like a Mellow Mushroom super fan. The founder said, "So that would make you the Number One Mellow Mushroom Super Fan." Does that make it official? I'd like to think so.

Why did you decide to start visiting Mellow Mushroom locations, and how many have you visited?
When I walked into a Mellow Mushroom, I was mesmerized by how different it was from a normal pizza joint. Great tunes and colorful decor give it such a groovy atmosphere. I loved everything about it. The second Mellow I visited was just as cool, but completely different. At that point I had the "got to see them all" inspiration, and I've been

visiting locations ever since. I have visited eighty-three locations and have one hundred sixty left to go. One day I would like to say that I've visited them all.

How does the rest of your family feel about your pizza adventures?
I feel their love and support on every Mellow adventure. They have been right there with me every time, and I think they would feel left out if they weren't there. Gathering my family around a couple of pizzas for some good quality time together is one of my favorite things, but at times I'm sure they think it's a little cheesy (no pun intended).

What is your favorite type of pizza?
All pizza is good, but I prefer a traditional pizza, with high-quality ingredients and a lot of cheese. Ham was the first added topping I ever tried, and it's probably my favorite topping, but don't tell bacon I said that.

Why pizza?
Because of its ooey gooey cheesiness and its shareability. Pizza is awesome!

Can you remember your first pizza as a kid?
I was probably about four years old, and I went with my mother to go pick up a pizza for dinner. I actually got to ride with it on my lap on the way home. The delicious aroma of that pizza is something I will never forget.

A Mellow Mushroom in Chattanooga, Tennessee.

Detroit-Style Pizza with Pepperoni

Recipe courtesy of Shawn Randazzo, owner of Detroit Style Pizza Company in Clinton Township, Saint Claire Shores, and Roseville, Michigan.

- 1 c. water (90–95 degrees Fahrenheit)
- 1 tsp. sugar
- 1/2 tsp. instant dry yeast (IDY)
- 2 c. all-purpose or bread flour (bread flour recommended)
- 1 tsp. salt
- 1–2 oz. vegetable oil
- 32 pieces pepperoni
- 12 oz. mozzarella or pizza cheese (a mozzarella/brick cheese blend is traditionally used)
- 4–5 oz. pizza sauce

Instructions

Place water into a 16 oz. glass or cup. Add sugar and IDY and mix with spoon or fork thoroughly for 15–20 seconds. Let sit for 5–10 minutes. Stir water, mix one last time and pour into a mixing bowl, adding flour and salt.

Using kitchen mixer, mix on low for about 2 minutes. (If mixing by hand, use an oiled spoon [preferably wooden] and mix well, 40 times around until dough clumps up into a ball.)

Using oiled hands, knead the dough ball by folding over and pressing down hard, repeating about 20 times. If making a large 10x14-size pizza, make into a dough ball and lightly coat the entire dough ball with oil and place back in bowl. If making two 8x10 small pizzas, divide the dough ball evenly and make two small dough balls, then lightly coat with oil and set back in bowl.

Oil a 10x14 or two 8x10 Detroit-style pizza pans (or a rectangular pan with raised edges). Place dough into 10x14 or two 8x10 pans. Using a little oil to coat your hand, again press dough into pan until consistently even throughout. If dough keeps pulling back and won't fully press out, cover and put aside for 15 minutes and come back to it.

Once dough is pressed out evenly throughout entire pan, you can start topping your dough or let dough proof by covering with a pan lid and setting aside at room temperature for 1–3 hours (the longer you let it proof, the better the texture and thicker and airier your pizza will be).

Traditionally, pepperoni is placed on the dough first, next comes the cheese, and lastly, the sauce is ladled on top either before or after baking.

Preheat oven to 450 degrees Fahrenheit and bake pizza for 15 minutes (17 minutes if you decide to add more toppings). To check doneness, look for a golden bottom crust and use a fork to check middle of pizza to make sure dough is fully cooked. Using pan grippers (or sturdy tongs) and a spatula, work the baked pizza out of its pan and onto a cutting board. Let sit for a minute to cool, cut into square slices, and serve.

A **PAN GRIPPER** is a tool used to remove hot pizza pans from the oven.

CATSUP IN FLAVORS!

New from Hunt's—New Hickory Flavor Catsup for that special barbecue flavor, and New Pizza Flavor Catsup to add that Italian accent. Both great on everything you use catsup on! Both from Hunt's...the catsup with the Big Tomato Taste.

ABOVE: Can you imagine that something this delicious was once thought to be poisonous?

LEFT: Pizza and tomatoes are a match made in food paradise—so much so that they've even inspired pizza-flavored catsup.

CHAPTER NINE

SAUCES AND SPICES

Flatbreads sans tomato have been eaten since further back in history than we can document, but part of what makes pizza a pizza is the sauce.

Tomatoes were discovered in 1522, when Spanish conquistadors came upon them growing in the Peruvian Andes. Unfortunately, when the new fruit was brought back to Europe, everyone was too scared to eat it. The rumor was that tomatoes were poisonous. Only the poor were brave enough to try out the fear-inducing fruit; once tomatoes were found to be harmless, everyone began integrating them into their diets (mainly in pastas at first). Legend says that Italian sailors used to eat a lot of pasta with tomato sauce back in the sixteenth century. In fact, the word "marinara" originates from the Italian word "*marinaro*," which means "of the sea."

By the 1700s, tomatoes had made their way onto flatbreads and focaccia, the first step toward their role in the pizza sauce we all love today. By the time pizza was officially introduced to Americans in 1905, with the opening of Lombardi's, the tomato sauce was the star of the show. Many early pizzerias referred to their pizzas—and pizzerias—as tomato pie.

Since those early days of pizza, the humble tomato sauce has always remained a constant, even as pizza has changed around the country. Its simplicity is unmatched. Most chefs don't even need to cook a sauce, but rather hand crush a few plum tomatoes right onto the pie, along with some extra-virgin olive oil and seasoning. You can't argue with nature's perfection.

As pizzerias have looked to stand out over the past few decades, we've seen new sauces emerge on pizza, such as barbecue, ranch, garlic, Alfredo, and more. They're all interesting to try, but our taste buds usually lead us

Pizza makers use all kinds of methods to apply sauce to a pizza. Some, like Jonathan Goldsmith (top right) of Spacca Napoli in Chicago, use small spoons; others, like the original De Lorenzo's Tomato Pies in Trenton, New Jersey (top left), or J&V Pizzeria in Brooklyn (bottom right), use ladles. Some, like L&B Spumoni Gardens in Brooklyn (bottom left), use wooden spoons that help to smooth the sauce on large pies. Still others use their bare hands to crush the tomatoes and place them directly on the pizza. *DeLorenzo's photo courtesy of DeLorenzo's*

back to the traditional tomato-based sauce we grew up enjoying.

In those sauces or scattered on our pizzas, some herbs and spices have become typical over the years. These include basil, oregano, garlic, and red pepper flakes.

Sweet basil, part of the mint family, has been closely associated with pizza since the story began as well. It's often found in full-leaf form on top of a Margherita pizza, chopped up and used as a garnish on other types of pizzas, or mixed into tomato sauces at the last moment, lending an aromatic scent and a sweet flavor to any recipe. Basil most likely originated in Asia and Africa, before Alexander the Great brought it to Greece. It arrived in Europe, through India, in the sixteenth century and eventually made it to America in the seventeenth century. A legend in Italy claims that sweet basil attracts husbands and wives to one another. Maybe Queen Margherita quite literally fell in love with the pizza that Raffaele Esposito created for her!

Oregano is one of those spices you'll find in almost every pizzeria, which is why it's nicknamed the "pizza herb." Some pizzerias mix it in their sauces, while others toss a dash or two on top of the cheese before the pie goes in to bake. Although oregano has been

TOP: In situations like this one, there are usually arguments over who will get the basil.
BOTTOM: Dom DeMarco of Di Fara Pizza, in Brooklyn, grows his own basil in a windowsill and hand cuts it onto each pie as it comes out of the oven.

in use since the seventh century BC to flavor proteins, vegetables, and wine (and was used even earlier for medicinal purposes), no one began growing it in America until colonial times. Its widespread use did not occur until after World War II, when soldiers returned from Europe with a taste for it.

No one knows the exact origin of **garlic**, but records trace it back five thousand years to China. Traders brought it with them to Egypt, India, and Europe. While peasants seemed to use it, garlic didn't sit so well with everyone—it's said that high-class society didn't like garlic because it caused bad breath and had a medicinal taste. Most often it was considered a peasant food, overlooked by serious cooks unless used in extreme moderation. Italians and the French kept it to sauces in the Middle Ages. Garlic is still used in relative moderation in Italian cooking.

Garlic first came to America via the Spaniards, who introduced it to

Pizza that is undercooked or has sauce seepage often falls prey to a **GUM LINE**, a gummy layer of dough that can appear between the crust and toppings.

the Choctaw Indians of Alabama, Louisiana, and Mississippi around 1500. The Indians began growing the spice in their gardens, and there it remained. It seems America wasn't too keen on garlic either. It wasn't until the 1950s, when chefs like James Beard and Craig Claiborne started introducing Americans to French cuisine incorporating garlic, that everyone started jumping on the garlic bandwagon.

What's interesting to note about this pungent, yet deliciously fragrant and flavorful, bulb, is that it's actually odorless. That's right. It's the cutting and smashing that causes a chemical reaction, which creates the familiar garlic smell none of us wants on our breath.

Crushed red pepper flakes, those hot little numbers you find in shakers on

A simple focaccia is perfect with olive oil, garlic, and oregano.

pizzeria tabletops all over America, are a mix of several dried peppers including ancho, cayenne, bell, and others. You won't find this spice mix in pizzerias in Italy. Many of the first pizzerias to open in America, including Lombardi's in New York and Papa's Tomato Pies in New Jersey, have been offering red pepper flakes since day one. History indicates that Italians, notably southern Italians, have always appreciated spicy foods, so when those same Italians opened pizzerias in America, they offered a spice mix that would please their fellow Italians. The tradition has carried on here in America, although for some unknown reason it has died off in southern Italy.

A Margherita pizza brings sauce and basil together in the most delicious way.

EXTRA TOPPING

Marinara will probably always be our number-one choice for sauce, but you can't argue with Elvis Presley. One of The King's favorite pizzas in Memphis, Tennessee, was the BBQ Pizza from Coletta's Restaurant, which originated the pie topped with pulled pork, barbecue sauce, and cheese during the 1950s. It's still one of the restaurant's top sellers, with many customers choosing to eat one while sitting at the table where Elvis sat.

Pizza fit for The King.

CHAPTER TEN

A St. Louis-style pie. *J. Pollack Photography / jpollackphoto.com*

ST. LOUIS STYLE

ST. LOUIS STYLE

How to Recognize It

Right off the bat, you'll notice the fact that this round pie is cut into squares (called a "party cut" regionally). It's super thin all the way around—there's no raised crust—with toppings that stretch out to the edges of the pizza. The sauce leans toward sweet, and it's almost always topped with Provel, a regionally available cheese manufactured from cheddar, Swiss, provolone, and liquid smoke.

Where to Find It

This style is most common in Missouri, mostly because of the regionally available Provel cheese. However, local chain Imo's Pizza has been opening locations in Illinois and Kansas over the years, exposing a new audience to the style. Most other pizzerias serving St. Louis-style pizza outside of the state usually have Provel shipped in or mimic it in the kitchen by combining cheddar, Swiss, and smoked provolone.

In the 1950s, Italian immigrants began settling in an area of St. Louis called The Hill. This is the first area where pizzerias began to open in the city, and it's still known for its Italian-influenced bakeries and restaurants.

St. Louis teenagers on a date, 1957. *Time & Life Pictures / Getty Images*

While Imo's Pizza is widely recognized as the pizzeria that put St. Louis style on the map, legend says that Ed and Margie Imo were not the originators of the style. Farotto's, another historic pizzeria in St. Louis, opened its doors in 1956, and according to an interview with former owner Jim Parrott prior to his 2013 passing, it was his parents who debuted the St. Louis style.

The pizza's shining star, for better or worse depending on who you ask, is the Provel cheese topping, which is said to have been created specifically for the pizza industry in 1947 by Costa Grocery (now Roma Grocery) and the Hoffman Dairy Company of Wisconsin (now part of Kraft Foods). Its characteristic stretch-less melt helps give St. Louis-style pizza its clean bite. I may be alone here, but I have a theory that Provel's liquid smoke ingredient was originally included to impart a smoky flavor reminiscent of the wood-burning ovens of Italy.

The pizza's thin crust is the result of yeast-free dough, which eliminates the rise that normally occurs before baking. This also saves a lot of prep

CORNICIONE is a fancy word for the outer edge of a pizza crust.

J. Pollack Photography / jpollackphoto.com

Some regions of the country take a thin-crust round pizza and cut it into squares, called a **PARTY CUT** or **TAVERN CUT**. Squares are much easier to eat when holding a beer.

time in the kitchen, perhaps a necessity for early adapters of the style. The St. Louis style is one of the fastest styles to bake at home, since there's no need to wait for the dough to rise.

Once you start eating St. Louis-style pizza, it's pretty hard to stop. The crust is so super thin that it's almost like eating cheese and crackers, but in a really good way.

"You better cut the pizza in four pieces because I'm not hungry enough to eat six."

—*Yogi Berra*

HOW TO MAKE IT

St. Louis-Style Pizza

Try this Imo's-inspired recipe from King Arthur Flour recipe creator PJ Hamel.

Yield: two pizzas, about 4 servings total

2 c. unbleached self-rising flour
(No self-rising flour? Substitute 2 cups all-purpose flour, add 1 tsp. baking powder and $1/2$ tsp. salt, and increase water to $1/2$ c.)

2 tbsp. olive oil

6 tbsp. water

$2/3$ c. pizza sauce

1 c. sharp white cheddar cheese, grated or shredded

$1/2$ c. smoked provolone cheese, grated or shredded (To add smoky flavor without using smoked provolone, add 1 tsp. liquid smoke flavoring)

$1/2$ c. Swiss cheese, grated or shredded

Pizza seasoning or dried Italian herbs

Instructions

Preheat the oven to 425 degrees Fahrenheit. Lightly grease two 12-inch round pizza pans, or a couple of baking sheets.

Combine the flour, oil, and water, mixing until cohesive. Gather the dough into a ball, divide it in half, and shape each half into a flat disk, the rounder the better. If you have time, let the dough rest, covered, for 10 to 15 minutes; it'll be easier to roll out once it's rested.

Grease a piece of parchment paper about 12 inches square, or a piece of waxed paper or plastic wrap. Place one of the dough pieces on the paper, and top with another piece of lightly greased parchment, waxed paper, or plastic wrap. Roll the dough very thin, ⅛" thick or less.

Place the pizzas on the prepared pans. Top each pizza with ⅓ c. of the sauce.

Mix the cheeses together and spread half over each pizza. Sprinkle lightly with pizza seasoning or dried Italian herbs.

Bake the pizzas for 9 to 11 minutes, until the cheese is melted and beginning to brown, and the edges and bottom of the crust are golden brown.

Remove the pizzas from the oven, transfer to a rack to cool very briefly, cut in squares, and serve hot.

ST. LOUIS-STYLE PIZZA FOUND OUTSIDE ITS NATURAL HABITAT

5th Street Pizza, Allen, TX, 5thstreetpizza.net

Arch Pizza, Denver, CO, archpizzaco.com

City Pizza & Pasta, Arvada, CO, citypizzaandpasta.com

Michael's Pizzeria, Easley, SC, michaelspizzeria.org

Speedy Romeo, Brooklyn, NY, speedyromeo.com

STEVE GREEN

Steve Green is the Oxford, Mississippi-based publisher of *PMQ Pizza Magazine*.

Steve Green. *Courtesy* PMQ Pizza Magazine.

As the publisher of America's number one pizza trade publication, you've been able to see the industry grow firsthand. What has that growth looked like over the past ten years?
Because the pizza industry is such a mature industry here in the United States, we have many concepts and styles that have sprouted and are doing well, including fast casual, take-and-bake, Neapolitan, and more. Even the economic crisis of 2008 couldn't stop consumers from having their pizza. Instead, it gave rise to lower-cost pizzas, bundled promotions, and specials.

Do you feel like the popularity of pizza has increased?
Yes! Internationally speaking, it has absolutely increased. The reason we have a publication in China now is because we had so many people from China coming to our website to learn about the pizza business. The same goes for Australia, Brazil, Russia, and the Middle East. In countries where there is no Italian base, such as Russia, you see more American-style pizza.

How do today's pizzerias compare to one five or ten years ago? How have they changed with the times?
Being a former Domino's franchisee, I can remember when we were only allowed to sell pizza—no sides or sandwiches. Since then, consumers have grown to expect more. Menu expansion has proliferated in the industry, and pizza has become so popular that restaurants outside of the pizza realm now carry pizza on the menu. However, there will always be a home for the pizza craftsman, and those who want the best will go to a pizzeria. People have an emotional connection to pizza, which doesn't exist with other foods.

How does today's pizza consumer compare to the consumer from five or ten years ago?
Today's consumer knows more about pizza thanks to TV, magazines, books, the expansion of the industry, more sophisticated tastes, etc.

EXTRA TOPPING

Each person in America eats close to fifty slices of pizza each year.

Coming to a DVD player near you: in 2013, Domino's Brazil teamed up with video rental stores and created DVDs with thermal ink. The ink heats up inside your DVD player, and when the movie is over and you pop out the DVD, the image—and smell—of pizza appears, along with a message to enjoy your next movie with a pizza.

Italy and France have a culture of food, while America has a culture of convenience. But this culture has helped to bring about the changes that our industry needed to make in order to stay ahead of today's sophisticated—and hurried—consumer.

How does the American pizza industry compare to that of other countries?
I think that Alex Platzl, CEO of Pizza Mann, Austria, summed it up best when he told me, "Pizza is Italian, but the pizza business is American."

Many people are surprised to hear that there's a pizza magazine that's been around for more than fifteen years. What inspires you to stay involved in the industry?
It's such a fun business to be in! People seem to have a natural-born, emotionally reinforced connection to pizza that they've been nurturing their entire lives, so it's about half as difficult to market pizza as any other product. The demographics for pizza are the same as oxygen breathers—pretty much one hundred percent. I really love the people in the pizza business, too. They are all people who want to serve others

and truly love what they do, despite being challenged every day and on so many different levels. I like that wherever I go in the world, I can find pizza. I can walk into a pizzeria thousands of miles away and find similar equipment, a pizzaiolo creating his pies, and smiling customers. The setting is familiar, but the stories are different. The chance to meet [new people] and learn new things about this business every day, and to share that knowledge with my readers so that they can become more successful, is what keeps me going.

Do you have any childhood pizza memories?
Back around 1964, my father used to attend monthly business meetings with a group of associates at a pizzeria. Each time they met, they carried a sign that said "Pizza Club of America." I was too young to join them, but my older brother always got to go, which, I'll admit, made me a little jealous. I ended up in the pizza business and my brother didn't, but let's not read too much into that.

Pizza at the organic chain Pizza Fusion is the epitome of the California style.

CHAPTER ELEVEN

CALIFORNIA
STYLE

CALIFORNIA STYLE

How to Recognize It

This style focuses on toppings rather than crust. Topping examples that can tip you off to a California-style pizza include fresh produce (heirloom tomatoes, asparagus, avocado, broccoli), locally sourced cheeses, atypical proteins (duck, mussels, lobster), and any toppings that you would consider "organic" in nature. Sauces other than marinara (barbecue sauce, garlic sauce, olive oil) are often used, and internationally themed pizzas (Thai pizza, Mexican pizza) are identifiable as members of the California-style family as well.

Where to Find It

California style is one of the more recent pizza styles to be introduced, inspired by gourmet dishes and locally sourced ingredients. You can find it all over California, and now it's also appearing across the rest of the country, since so many pizzerias are integrating fresh herbs, locally sourced meats and cheeses, and sometimes wild toppings to make their pizza stand out.

Just like chefs in every other region, California chefs used what they had available to them when first experimenting with pizza. Because of the climate, fresh produce is available almost year round, so why not

ABOVE: Sprouts, avocado, and nuts: the quintessential healthy California-style pie.
ABOVE RIGHT and RIGHT: Not all California-style pizzas are found in California. These slices were spotted in New York.

rate it into pizza and make it a gourmet offering? It may not appeal to die-hard New York-style fans, but the California style definitely has a following.

There are several names that come to mind when we think about the history of California-style pizza: Alice Waters, Ed LaDou, and Wolfgang Puck. All three chefs had a hand in bringing California-style pizza to consumers in the early 1980s.

Originally from New Jersey, Alice Waters received a degree in French cultural studies from the University of California, Berkeley. It was during a study abroad trip to France that she was exposed to cooking with local produce. She brought the love of local foods back to the States with her and opened Chez Panisse in Berkeley in 1967, for which she created gourmet menus using locally sourced products. In 1980, she opened Chez Panisse Café directly above the original restaurant, offering pizzas cooked in a wood-fired oven and integrating some of the gourmet ingredients already being featured in the main restaurant below, such as grilled radicchio, leeks, duck confit, quail eggs, mussels, crawfish tails, and wild mushrooms.

Meanwhile, another chef was doing some experimenting of his own. Ed LaDou, who had been working in pizzerias since he was nineteen years old, had been topping pizzas with ingredients like eggplants and clams at a restaurant called Prego in San

ABOVE: Pizza Brain in Philadelphia, Pennsylvania, is serving up some pretty spectacular California-style slices.
BELOW: Alice Waters makes pizzas with Prince Charles and Camilla, Duchess of Cornwall, in 2005. *Associated Press*

Ed LaDou in 2007, with a grilled eggplant, goat cheese, and arugula pie. *Associated Press*

Francisco. In 1980, Wolfgang Puck tried one of LaDou's pizzas while dining at the restaurant. It was topped with ricotta cheese, red peppers, pâté, and mustard. Puck immediately offered LaDou a job as the pizza chef at the not-yet-opened Spago.

When Spago opened in Beverly Hills in 1982, LaDou was creating pizzas topped with smoked salmon, duck sausage, and anything else he wanted to serve up to the celebrity clientele. The pizza was in high demand, and it gave two other entrepreneurs an idea.

PIZZA PIONEERS

- Gennaro Lombardi opened America's first pizzeria in New York in 1905. Lombardi's, just a few doors away from its original location, is still open today.
- The table-shaped "pizza saver" you've seen, which protects pizzas from getting smashed by their boxes, was invented by Carmela Vitale in 1985.
- Pizzeria operators Rose and Jim Totino began a frozen pizza business in 1962. It was purchased by Pillsbury in 1981.
- Ingrid Kosar received a patent for the pizza thermal bag in 1984 and signed her first major contract with Domino's Pizza the same year, helping to revolutionize the pizza delivery business and ensuring that we all receive our pizzas hot on arrival.
- In 1933, Patsy Lancieri (of Patsy's Pizzeria in New York) was the first pizzeria operator to offer pizza by the slice. Operators prior to him had served pizzas whole, and many continued to afterward, wanting to stick with tradition. Americans, however, embraced the new portable slices.
- Pizza Inn, based in The Colony, Texas, invented the first dessert pizza, named the "pizzert," in 1986. Pizzerts are still offered, with traditional toppings such as a fruit of the day, chocolate chips, or Bavarian crème.

Larry Flax and Rick Rosenfield, two Los Angeles attorneys, decided they wanted to bring gourmet pizza to the masses after Flax took one of LaDou's pizza-making classes. LaDou was hired by Flax and Rosenfield to create the menu for California Pizza Kitchen, which has grown to more than two hundred fifty locations since its 1985 founding and still features many of LaDou's early creations, including the popular BBQ chicken pizza.

The original BBQ Chicken Pizza at California Pizza Kitchen.

- The French-bread pizzas you enjoy from the local grocery store freezer were the brainchild of Bob Petrillose, who began selling what he called "poor man's pizza" (pizza on French bread) out of a food truck he dubbed the "Hot Truck." Petrillose sold the pizzas on the campus of Cornell University in Ithaca, New York, from 1960 to 2000.

- The process of creating frozen pizza was issued a patent on February 2, 1954, to inventor Joseph Bucci.

- Charles and Max Fleischmann introduced America to the first commercially produced yeast in 1868.

- Ira Nevin introduced the gas-fired pizza oven to America in the late 1940s, allowing pizza-making to be easier for anyone interested in getting into the business.

- The first pizza chain, Pizza Hut, was started in 1958 by Frank and Dan Carney in Wichita, Kansas. By 1960, there were twenty-five Pizza Hut stores; today, there are more than eleven thousand locations worldwide.

MARK BELLO

Mark Bello is the owner of Pizza a Casa Pizza School (pizzaschool.com) in New York City.

Mark Bello. *Photograph by Lou Manna*

For several years now, you've been teaching people how to make pizza in their homes. Where did you come up with the idea to open a pizza school, and how many people have taken your course?

I grew up in New York and New Jersey. When I attended graduate school in Chicago, I found myself in a land of deep-dish and dismal fast-food pizzas, so I took to my kitchen and endeavored to create a recipe for perfect thin-crust pizza baked in a home oven. Long story short, friends started to notice, and then friends of friends started to notice. There was ever increasing demand for pizza knowledge. Here I am, almost twenty years later, running a specialty home-pizza school in New York City! A conservative estimate of how many people have taken my course is fifteen thousand and counting.

What is your background in the pizza industry?

I am a self-taught pizza maker first and foremost. I have a lot of friends in the biz and have done some time in front of professional ovens—everything from decks to wood-fired. The legit pizzas I've made in those settings, from the classic New York slice to a puffy/charred pie made in a wood-fired oven, are a testament to the "pizza sensibilities" I teach in my class, which provide the intel and instincts any pizza maker needs when faced with any oven format.

What are the most important points to remember when trying to make good pizza at home?

Less is more. Use better ingredients and you can use less. Let single flavors shine and simple combos harmonize. Heaping on toppings compromises the baking/crisping of your crust. Crank your oven as hot as it goes on "bake" and keep that door shut! Peeking at your pizza every thirty seconds causes the temperature in the oven to plummet, and your pies don't bake nearly as nicely.

What do you tell those who are afraid to try their hand at making pizza?

Fear not the yeast. People are most afraid of screwing up the dough. And it's not an unfounded fear, as there is/are a lot of information/recipes out there that don't really tell you how to do it. Failed attempts reinforce this fear. We are all about taking the fear out of dough-making and making it foolproof and fun.

Are there some basic tools you suggest using, if someone is going to bake pizza at home?

I recommend a good-quality pizza stone and peel or, in a pinch, a simple pizza screen.

In your opinion, what is the best way to reheat leftover pizza?

I made a video about the best and worst ways to reheat leftover pizza at slicemagic.com. The worst ways involve reheating in the microwave or oven, and the best use a preheated skillet and some foil.

Have you seen an increase in the number of consumers interested in making their own pizzas over the past several years? If yes, why do you think that is?

Yes. We get so many emails from alumni sharing stories of how pizza night has become a cherished tradition with friends and family. It just multiplies exponentially. We also launched an iPad app at diypizzapie.com that has recipes and videos to help create your own pizzas at home.

Have any of your students gone on to open pizzerias?

A bunch. Everywhere from New York City to New Jersey to the Midwest to Dubai, Singapore, Guyana, Mexico City, and the list goes on

EXTRA TOPPING

Since the 1980s, New York locals have linked the cost of a slice of pizza to the cost of a subway fare. They call it the Pizza Connection or the Pizza Principle. When the price of one goes up, invariably, so does that of the other.

HOW TO MAKE IT

Fig and Prosciutto White Pizza

Recipe by Brad Kent, executive chef,
Olio Pizzeria & Cafe, Los Angeles

(NOTE: For your crust, use either the Neapolitan-style dough recipe
on page 23 or the NY-style dough recipe found on page 50.)

240 g. dough ball,
  stretched or rolled to 13 inches

California extra virgin olive oil (enough for
brushing crust and drizzling after bake)

1½ tsp. Grana Padano cheese, freshly grated

2 California figs, quartered

6 heaping tsp. burrata cheese

6 slices fresh prosciutto or speck ham

¼ c. fresh baby wild arugula

1½ tsp. balsamic glaze (cook balsamic vinegar
  over low heat until slightly thickened)

Malden sea salt, to taste

Pepper, to taste

Instructions

Preheat oven on highest temperature setting for at least 40 minutes, with pizza stone closest to the bottom heat source. Brush pizza dough with olive oil and sprinkle with Grana Padano. Dock the crust with a fork to prevent it from rising in the center. Bake on preheated pizza stone approximately 4 minutes or until crust just begins to brown. Remove crust from oven and place fig quarters in a pinwheel fashion around the perimeter. Spoon dollops of burrata next to each fig quarter. Set pizza back in the oven to warm the burrata and figs for approximately 1 minute or up to 90 seconds (do not melt the burrata). Remove pizza from oven and cut into 6 slices. Lace sliced prosciutto or speck ham around the pizza. Garnish with fresh baby wild arugula, a drizzle of balsamic glaze and extra virgin olive oil. Finish with a light sprinkle of Malden sea salt and two turns of fresh ground black pepper.

ABOVE: Coal-fired ovens have a separate chamber to hold the coal, as seen here at Sally's Apizza in New Haven, Connecticut.

LEFT: A modern oven with coal inside.

CHAPTER TWELVE

OVENS

As you've gone through the book and read about the different pizza styles, you've probably noticed mentions of wood-burning ovens, coal-fired ovens, etc. These different ovens cook pizzas differently, and also require certain skill sets to operate.

Italians were used to cooking with wood, but when they arrived in America, coal was the only source of fuel that was affordable at the time. Early bakeries and pizzerias all used coal-burning ovens, which took a lot of work to maintain. It wasn't until much later, in the late 1940s, that oven manufacturer Bakers Pride introduced a gas-fired pizza oven, making it easy for hundreds of new pizzerias to open their doors.

Let's take a look at some of the most common oven types and what kinds of pizzas are typically produced in them.

Coal-Fired Oven–In an oven that uses coal for its main fuel source, the coal is typically placed in an adjoining oven compartment, which can reach temperatures of 2,000 degrees Fahrenheit. The heat is then transferred to the brick oven floor, where temperatures hover between 600 and 1,000 degrees. The interiors have thick brick hearths and walls, with a domed top that helps to retain and bounce back the heat. These ovens can take days to heat up

Manning the oven at DeLorenzo's Tomato Pies in Trenton, New Jersey. *Photo courtesy of DeLorenzo's*

ABOVE: Look at all of those stacked deck ovens! They were clearly pushing out a lot of pies at Aurelio's in Chicago. *Photo courtesy of Aurelio's*
LEFT: A standard brick oven at Original Presto's in West New York, New Jersey.

if they're starting from a cold state. Modern coal-burning ovens, which have seen a resurgence in the past five years, use gas burners to ignite the coals, which helps heat things up in a few hours. These ovens are still usually left burning at all times.

The anthracite coals used in most coal-fired ovens must be measured carefully to ensure there are enough to cook the pizzas, but not so much that the pizzas are scorched (coal delivers double the heat of wood). You'll see coal-fired ovens mostly in historic pizzerias, such as Lombardi's, Totonno's, and Patsy's in New York, and Pepe's and Sally's in New Haven.

Deck/Brick Oven–These ovens can be powered by electricity or gas and are lined with tiles, bricks, or stone. They're some of the most common ovens you'll find in mom-and-pop-type pizzerias and slice shops where there are only one or two people working with the ovens, since it often takes some skill to maneuver the pies and watch that none burn. Recent innovations eliminating the need to rotate the pizza during baking have made it easier for inexperienced cooks to handle this style of oven.

Conveyor Oven—A conveyor oven is an electric oven, which is designed for "no-mistakes" pizza baking. These were created in the 1980s to help grow franchise pizzerias that needed something everyone could use, for consistency. With a conveyor oven, you simply set the temperature and the time and place the uncooked pizza on one end of the metal belt. The pizza takes a ride through the oven and exits the other side fully cooked. These ovens are found in most chain pizzerias (the first of which, Pizza Hut, started in 1958) and high-production pizza stores, where many different staff members are in charge of making the pizzas.

Air Impingement Oven—The technology used in this type of oven was adapted from that used to cook for

TOP: This deck oven at Pizza Rev in Los Angeles has a gas flame on the side that can be used alone or with wood to bake pizzas.
BOTTOM: Conveyor ovens changed the industry by making baking as easy as placing a pizza on a conveyor belt.

EXTRA TOPPING

A central commissary often helps with consistency at multi-location pizzerias. The same dough, sauce, cheese, and other ingredients are shipped out to all pizza shops from one location, and staff at each store simply assembles and bakes the pies.

astronauts at NASA. It takes a normal conveyor oven and adds a shot of hot air above and below the pizza to eliminate moisture as it goes through the oven. The result is a pizza that cooks in less time, with a crisper crust.

Wood-Burning Oven—Wood-burning ovens may be the ones you're most familiar with since they're featured most prominently in the media, with their often glamorously tiled exteriors and trance-inducing flickering flames. Wood-burning ovens cook Neapolitan-style pizzas at temperatures topping 900 degrees Fahrenheit. In traditional wood-burning ovens, the wood is the only source of heat, but modern times call for modern solutions, and many of the ovens you see now also get a little help from a gas flame. Hard woods, such as mesquite, pecan, cherry, and oak, are the most common types used, as they have a low smoke and give off the most heat.

The act of partially baking a pizza dough, with no toppings added, is called **PARBAKING**.

Wood-burning ovens like this one at Spacca Napoli in Chicago require a constant supply of wood and a skilled pizzaiolo to man the oven at all times.

Cooking the same type of pizza in different types of ovens will deliver different results, mainly in the char characteristics on the top and bottom of the pizza. For this reason, pizzeria operators normally explore several options before choosing the oven that will consistently deliver the type of pizza they want to make.

Over the years, ovens have continued to evolve to keep up with pizza's growing pains, but the oven type matters far less than the people creating the pizza—and those who decide to share it with one another.

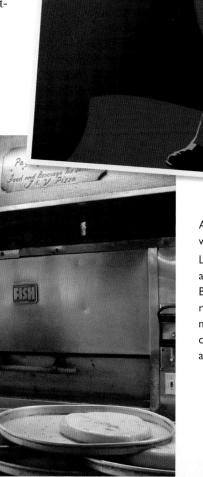

ABOVE: Ad with a wood-burning oven.

LEFT: This oven at J&V Pizzeria in Brooklyn has a rotating deck inside, making it possible to cook dozens of pizzas at the same time.

ABOVE: Stylish pizza (oh, the 1980s). © *Daily Mail / Rex / Alamy*
LEFT: Pizza (vocal) stylings.

MORE PIZZA STYLES!

B elieve it or not, we've only scratched the surface when it comes to pizza styles. Virtually every state you travel to in America will spotlight a different style of pizza in an effort to stand out from the pack. Here are a few you may—or may not—have heard about.

Bar/Tavern/Party-Cut Style–These pizzas are traditionally found in taverns and bars because they allow the customer to eat without filling up on dough (not to mention they're easy to hold while drinking a beer). The toppings and cheese are historically thin, and the round pies are cut into square slices. You'll see this style all over the Midwest, in places like Columbus, Ohio; St. Louis, Missouri (St. Louis style uses Provel cheese); Chicago, Illinois; and Milwaukee, Wisconsin. Pizza was the perfect bar food back in the 1950s. As business grew and pizza became more popular, some bars turned into pizzerias.

Grilled Pizza– Introduced to American palates in 1980 by Johanne Killeen and George German, the chef owners of Al Forno in Providence, Rhode Island, grilled pizza takes a well-oiled pizza dough and grills it on both sides over hot coals. Toppings are then added to finish it off.

They've been serving pizzas party-cut style at Rubino's Pizzeria in Columbus, Ohio, since 1954.

Stuffed Pizza–Found mostly in Chicago (Giordano's is an example), stuffed pizzas differ from deep-dish pizzas in that with a stuffed pizza, you get an extra (very thin) layer of crust over the toppings and under the top layer of sauce. This is often done to help keep the structural integrity of such a hefty pie.

Pan Pizza–This style gets its name from the dough being proofed and cooked in a pan. Oil in the pan gives the thick, finished pizza crust a light, buttery crunch. These pizzas are found in the southeastern United States. Chain pizzerias, such as Pizza Hut, offer them in other parts of the country.

Focaccia–This thick flatbread is one of the oldest styles of pizza. Often topped with olive oil, herbs, grilled vegetables, and cheeses, they can be found in bakeries and gourmet pizzerias.

TOP: Old Forge-style pizza from Arcaro & Genell in Old Forge, Pennsylvania. *Photo courtesy* PMQ Pizza Magazine
BOTTOM: *Photo courtesy* PMQ Pizza Magazine

A (quickly devoured) onion focaccia.

Old Forge Style–Hailing from "The Pizza Capital of The World" according to residents, the pizzas in Old Forge, Pennsylvania, are baked in trays, similar to Sicilian-style pizza. In lieu of calling them pizzas, pizzeria owners call the pies "trays," while slices are called "cuts." The sauce is heavy with onions and the cheese on top is usually mozzarella and cheddar or mozzarella and Parmesan.

The Montanara at Don Antonio by Starita in New York City.

Montanara–Introduced to the United States in 2007, the Montanara takes a Neapolitan-style dough and deep fries it before toppings are added. Several Neapolitan-style pizzerias, such as Forcella in New York, offer this style as a specialty item.

Vesuvio (or Bombe)–The Neapolitan answer to the stuffed-crust pizza, the Vesuvio puts two crusts on top of each other, filling the interior with items like mozzarella, tomatoes, or mushrooms. Each pizzeria serves it differently. Some, like Pizzeria da Nella in Chicago, bring the pie tableside and allow the steam from the joined doughs to escape, thus mimicking a volcanic eruption.

Tex-Mex–Found in the Southwest, this style contains 25 percent masa flour in its crust, giving it a corn chip flavor. Sauce is usually on the chunky side, and toppings range from shredded beef to corn and black beans.

Pizza Strips–A specialty of Rhode Island, pizza strips are bakery bread

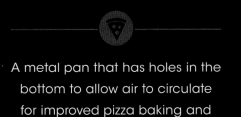

A metal pan that has holes in the bottom to allow air to circulate for improved pizza baking and browning is called a **SCREEN**.

that's been topped with tomato sauce and cut into strips. It's very similar to the Philly tomato pies you'd find in Pennsylvania, except these have been cut into strips instead of squares. Palmieri's Bakery in Providence has been baking them for more than one hundred years.

Greek-Style Pizza–Most prevalent in New England, but also found in Greek restaurants across the United States, Greek-style pizza has a round, puffy, oiled dough that crisps up in the pan. The tomato sauce is usually heavy with oregano, and the cheese (most commonly a mix of mozzarella and cheddar) is laid on thick.

Quad Cities-Style Pizza–As the name implies, this style is popular in the Quad Cities of Rock Island, Moline, and East Moline in Illinois, and Bettendorf and Davenport in Iowa. It has several unique characteristics that make it stand out, including a pizza dough that contains a heavy dose of dark-roasted brewer's malt, making it appear darker than other crusts and imparting a nutty, sweet taste. The sauce is thin and spicy, and the signature lean pork sausage is heavy on fennel and other spices. The sausage gets spread from edge to edge and

topped with cheese before the pizza is cut into strips—never slices—using giant, razor-sharp scissors.

Colorado-Style Mountain Pie–So far, I've only heard of this style coming out of the kitchens of a Colorado-based pizzeria named Beau Jo's, which has

A Greek pizza—with feta and tofu—is prepared at a Colorado yoga retreat. Denver Post *via Getty Images*

This slice at Big Mama's and Papa's Pizzeria in Hollywood is reminiscent of the jumbo D.C. slices. It's cut from a 36-inch pie.

served mountain pies since 1973. For hungry hikers and skiers in the region, the pizza is listed on the menu by weight instead of inches, is topped with mountains of ingredients, and features a hand-rolled crust edge that does indeed resemble a mountain. Leftover crust is traditionally dipped in honey and eaten as dessert. Beau Jo's has seven locations around Colorado and one in South Dakota.

Ohio Valley Pizza–In the Ohio Valley region, toppings are put on square pies after the dough comes out of the oven. Pizzerias such as Mario DiCarlo's Pizza in Wheeling, West Virginia, flash bake the dough in a brick oven, adding sauce, cheese, and toppings after the bake. The theory is that the heat from the crust will cook the toppings.

D.C. Jumbo Slices–Since 1997, several pizzerias in the Washington, D.C., area have been feuding over who offers the largest slices of pizza. Popular with late-night crowds, the slices are usually served

The slice, as American as the Boy Scouts.

MORE PIZZA STYLES!

133

Think you've seen everything? Here are a few pizzerias that are taking pizza beyond traditional toppings.

- The "Charlie Mayfer" at Pizza Brain in Philadelphia, Pennsylvania, is topped with mozzarella, sweet potatoes, Honeycrisp apples, honey goat cheese, brown sugar, pecans, and pie spice.

- The "caviar pizza" at Pravda in New York arrives topped with caviar, salmon, and red onions.

- Deep-fried pizza (yes, like the one you get at the fair) is available at the Chip Shop in Brooklyn.

- The "nutty idea pizza" at Roma Pizza in Greely, Colorado, is topped with pepperoni, tomatoes, cream cheese, mozzarella, and cashews.

- The "crab Rangoon pizza" at Fong's Pizza in Des Moines, Iowa, features a crab Rangoon base along with surimi, green onions, asiago, mozzarella, crispy egg roll strips, and sweet chili sauce.

- The "stroganoff pizza" at Bella Vista Brazilian Gourmet Pizza in Culver City, California, is topped with beef stroganoff and potato sticks.

- Apollonia's Pizzeria in Los Angeles has an exotic sausage menu. "The dirty agent" pie is topped with rattlesnake, alligator, or duck and bacon sausage.

- At Grinders in Kansas City, Missouri, any pizza can be made into a "chili bomb pie" with chili, cheese, Tater Tots (® by Ore-Ida), and scallions added to the center of your pie.

- Kono, which has 130 locations in 20 countries, offers a pizza in a cone at its first U.S. outpost in Edison, New Jersey, which opened in the summer of 2013. The pizzeria sells pizza dough in the shape of a cone, filled with ingredients from the traditional to breakfast, deli, and dessert varieties.

- For those looking for something a little different, Evan's Neighborhood Pizza in Fort Myers, Florida, has an "alligator pizza" with a blend of Florida alligator and spicy sausage.

"Lovers . . . oh, that word bums me out unless it's between 'meat' and 'pizza.'"

—*Liz Lemon*

on two plates and cut from pies that can be up to thirty inches across. Chris Chishti, who originated the jumbo slice at his first pizzeria, Pizza Mart, in the Adams Morgan neighborhood in 1997 (and now has a new shop, The Jumbo Slice), says that he came up with the idea after taking an unusable dough ball and mixing it with a fresh one to form one huge pizza. Several other pizzerias in the area began offering gigantic slices that can tip the scales at more than one thousand calories a piece.

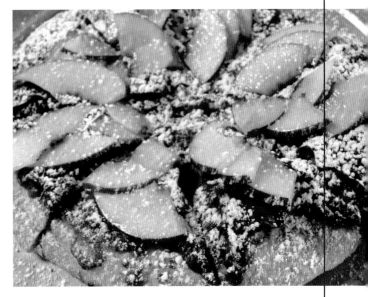

Nutella and peach dessert pizza at Tribecca Allie Café in Sardis, Mississippi.

Brier Hill Pizza–Here's a style that began in Youngstown, Ohio, with the help of St. Anthony's Catholic Church. The round pies are traditionally made in pans and covered with a thick sauce before being topped with bell peppers and Romano cheese. (A hot variety and one topped with eggs are also offered.) The church had been meeting the religious and community needs—many of which involved food—of Italian immigrants to Youngstown since the parish opened in 1898. It started offering the pizzas for sale once a week in 1974 as a fundraising project.

Dessert Pizza–Several pizza chains offer a sweet pizza to finish your meal; some offer much more elaborate dessert pizzas, if your taste buds lean

toward sweet. The decadent "midnight delight" at All Star Pizza Bar in Cambridge, Massachusetts, features buttered cinnamon-sugar pizza dough, caramelized banana purée, Johnny's cheesecake, Nutella hazelnut spread, marshmallows, fresh banana slices, and chocolate chips.

Breakfast Pizza–I'm not talking about cold leftovers from last night here. What began as a simple egg on top of a traditional pizza soon turned into pizzas featuring eggs, bacon, sausage, potatoes, and more, all offered during weekend brunch or even weekday breakfast. Pulino's Bar & Ristorante in New York, which shuttered in 2014, was one of the pioneers of the pizza brunch, serving pies topped with eggs

The "two boots" of Two Boots Pizza, founded in 1987 in the East Village of Manhattan, are Italy and Louisiana. The pizzeria specializes in Cajun-Italian cooking, as well as pop culture: pizzas are inspired by *The Big Lebowski*'s The Dude, *Seinfeld*'s Newman, and other probable pizza lovers. *The Jon B. Lovelace Collection of California Photographs in Carol M. Highsmith's America Project, Library of Congress*

alongside toppings like spinach, caramelized onions, mushrooms, mascarpone, pancetta, and sausage.

Hawaiian Pizza–Even though this pizza is topped with pineapple and ham, it originated more than four thousand miles away from the Aloha State, in Ontario, Canada. Sam Panopoulos, a Greek restaurateur with a Chinese restaurant, came up with the combination in 1962. A widespread tiki craze at the time helped the style, which offers salty and sweet satisfaction, take flight.

MELTING-POT PIZZA

Have you ever been to a restaurant and seen an unusual pizza that was inspired by another culture? Here are a few examples.

A full line of Indian-inspired pizzas can be found at Tasty Subs & Pizza in Sunnyvale, California, including a **Paneer Pizza**, which is made with Shahi paneer sauce, homemade paneer, mushrooms, red onions, bell peppers, tomatoes, garlic, mozzarella cheese, fresh cilantro, and diced red onion.

Shokudo Japanese Restaurant & Bar in Honolulu, Hawaii, has a **Sushi Pizza** on its menu, made by taking baked sushi rice and topping it with salmon, scallops, crabmeat, onions, and jalapeños.

For those looking for some South American flair, Buenos Aires Pizzeria in Denver, Colorado, has pizzas

 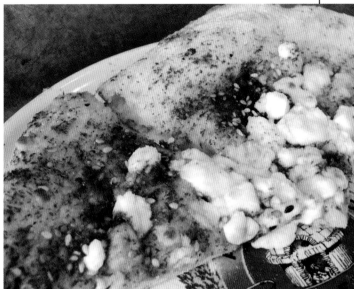

LEFT: The São Paulo at Piola in Hallandale Beach, Florida.
RIGHT: Za'tar-topped pizza.

like the **Buenos Aires**, topped with mozzarella, ham, hearts of palm, roasted red peppers, hard-boiled egg, and salsa. And Piola in Hallandale Beach, Florida, offers the **São Paulo**, topped with Catupiry cheese (popular in Brazil) and a dash of parsley.

Za'tar, a Middle Eastern spice mixture containing spices like thyme, oregano, marjoram, sumac, and sesame seeds, is often used to top pita bread, creating a pizza that is reminiscent of the flatbreads eaten in ancient Egypt.

A popular Turkish pizza, **Lahmacun**, is topped with minced meat, onions, and peppers and is available at many Middle Eastern restaurants.

Twin Rocks Café in Bluff, Utah, claims to have invented **Navajo Pizza**, a pizza that starts with crispy frybread, a Native American staple, and is topped with homemade tomato sauce and traditional pizza toppings.

Muslims abide by a strict dietary law called Halal, and it can be difficult to find pizza that meets those laws. **Halal Pizza** must not contain pork or pork products, such as lard, in its toppings, sauce, or dough. Because of this, it is often best to seek out a restaurant that is already serving Halal foods or a pizzeria that specifically offers Halal pizza, such as Anna's Pizza in Dearborn Heights, Michigan.

The Let's Pizza vending machine makes pizzas to order—inside the machine, the dough is mixed, the toppings are applied, and the pizza is cooked. A clever window allows you to watch the entire process, which takes just three minutes. The machines have been in use in Italy since 2009, and may turn up at a location near you soon.

New Yorkers, accustomed to inexpensive grab-and-go slices, were introduced to a $1,000 pizza in 2007, when New York City pizzeria Nino's Bellisima topped a pie with crème fraiche, four different types of caviar, thinly sliced Maine lobster tail, salmon roe, and wasabi.

It's no secret that President Obama likes pizza. However, one pizzeria visit in particular stood out. The president received a giant bear hug from six foot three pizzeria operator Scott Van Duzer at Big Apple Pizza & Pasta Italian Restaurant in Fort Pierce, Florida, in 2012. The Secret Service was not prepared for the show of affection, but the president took it all in stride.

In 2001, Pizza Hut successfully delivered a six-inch salami pizza to astronauts on the International Space Station, making it the first pizza delivery to outer space. It's said that Pizza Hut paid Russia around one million dollars to help pull off the promotional campaign.

Pizza mixed with politics during the 2012 presidential race when Herman Cain, former president and CEO of Godfather's Pizza, threw his hat in the Republican presidential ring.

And the Oscar goes to . . . Pizza! Host Ellen DeGeneres turned the spotlight on pizza when she ordered twenty pizzas from Big Mama's and Papa's Pizza in Los Angeles, for the celebrity-packed audience at the 2014 Academy Awards.

Macaulay Culkin, made famous by his pizza scene in *Home Alone*, formed a band called The Pizza Underground in 2012. The band spoofs songs by The Velvet Underground; song titles include "Pizza Gal" and "All the Pizza Parties."

Patrick Stewart, of *Star Trek* fame, mistakenly misled America into thinking he had never tried pizza before. He posted a photo of himself with pizza to Twitter in 2013 along with the caption, "My first ever pizza slice." Turns out he meant he had always eaten from a full pie, never a slice!

In a hilarious rant against Donald Trump and his New York pizza etiquette, talk show host Jon Stewart went on for eight minutes about the pizza shared between Trump and Sarah Palin during Palin's visit to New York in 2011. Most notable critiques pertained to the selection of the pizzeria, the stacking of slices, and Trump's use of a fork—considered a pizza crime by most New Yorkers.

Harkening back to the soldiers who helped to grow pizza's popularity in the 1950s, the military has now developed a slice of pepperoni pizza for soldiers' ready-to-eat kits (MREs) that can last up to three years. Pizza was the number one requested MRE, and in 2014 the U.S. Military Lab in Massachusetts figured out how to make it a reality.

In 2013, NASA awarded a $125,000 grant to Systems & Materials Research Corporation to build a 3D printer that could print food—specifically, pizza—for astronauts on long missions. The project was a success and the company is now looking to expand the technology. Who knows; we may see pizza printers in our local electronic store in the next five to ten years.

Pop star Katy Perry made a splash on Twitter in 2009—she tweeted a pic of herself in the bath-tub, with only a cheese pizza covering her midsection.

In the late 1990s, an inventor named Mark O'Brien introduced a freeze-dried pizza with a one-year shelf life called The Pizza Maker to America, with the help of the Michigan State University Agriculture Department.

Celebrities who worked in the pizza industry before they became famous include Stephen Baldwin, who was a pizzeria employee; Bill Murray, a former pizza maker; and Jean-Claude Van Damme, who delivered pizzas.

Several actors and celebrities have used their love of pizza to open their own pizzerias, including Cathy Moriarty, Peyton Manning, Maria Shriver, and Jamal Mashburn.

Since we love our dogs like family, they should have pizza too, right? That was the thinking behind the Heaven Scent Pizza, invented by Blissful Biscuits back in 2006. It's even packaged in a pizza delivery box so Fido can feel like he's part of the pizza party.

In 2010, Joe Carrazza's Café in Victoria, Australia, collectively grossed folks out by topping pizzas with locusts, in an effort to ease the town's locust epidemic. Thankfully, this trend did not make it to the United States.

In 2013, Fat Boys reissued their debut 1984 album (which featured a photo of them standing on a pizza) in the shape of a pizza, and packaged in a pizza delivery box.

As is tradition for visitors to New York, when Governor George W. Bush came to New York in 1999, Mayor Rudolph Giuliani gave him a tour of the city that ended on Arthur Avenue in the Bronx, at a pizzeria called Giovanni's. In 2007, it was later revealed that President Bush's favorite dinner was homemade cheeseburger pizzas. ·

ABOVE: A button from Papa John's, a bumpersticker from Domino's, and a New Zealand Pizza Hut matchbook from the 1960s.

LEFT: Many pizzerias give out free items to help promote the brand, such as this light-up yo-yo from Shakey's.

CHAPTER FOURTEEN

ENTER THE CHAINS

Until now, we've focused mainly on the independently owned mom-and-pop bakeries, bars, and pizza shops that first introduced us to pizza. But if it weren't for the franchising of pizzerias during the 1960s and 1970s, pizza may not have spread so quickly throughout America.

Pizza chains today are big business, making up almost half of the seventy thousand-plus pizzerias in the United States. We know that the top three chains are Pizza Hut, Domino's, and Papa John's, but where did they get their starts, and who was first?

In 1954, **Shakey's Pizza Parlor & Ye Public House** opened in Sacramento, California, founded by Sherwood "Shakey" Johnson and Ed Plummer. The first store was so successful, with its live banjo and its player pianos, that a second store was opened in Portland, Oregon, in 1956. The following year, Shakey's became one of the first foodservice companies to begin franchising, a process that previously was really only relegated to car dealerships.

Success continued, and there were nearly three hundred stores by the end of the 1960s. Johnson retired in 1967 and Plummer sold his interest in the pizzeria in 1968. There are currently fifty-seven Shakey's Pizza and Buffet restaurant locations around the United States.

141

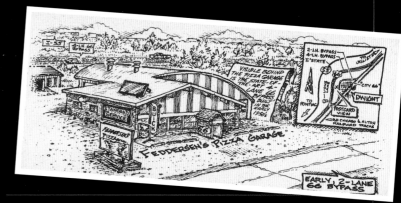

A 1930s Illinois car dealership-turned-Route 66 "pizza garage."

"There's no better feeling in the world than a warm pizza box on your lap."

—Kevin James

Pizza Hut, currently America's number one chain, with more than six thousand stores throughout the United States, began in Wichita, Kansas, in 1958—thanks to a six hundred-dollar loan from a loving mom who believed in her sons. Brothers Frank and Dan Carney wanted to start a business and had heard that pizza was a growing trend. They got help from their sister's neighbor, John Bender, who had worked at a pizzeria and was able to teach them how to make pizzas. It was rough going at first, but business took off quickly once they started letting customers sample the pies. Each time they had enough money, the brothers would open another store. The third store was a franchised store. Fees were extremely low to open a franchise (just one hundred dollars for the franchise and one hundred dollars per month maximum), resulting in one thousand Pizza Hut locations by 1972. In 1973, Dan left the business and Frank took over. He continued to grow the brand at a rapid clip. In 1977, the company was sold to PepsiCo, and it later spun off to YUM! Brands. Frank Carney, who loved the pizza business, eventually moved on to help a rival pizza chain, overseeing operations for dozens of Papa John's locations.

Little Caesars was founded in 1959 when Michael and Marian Ilitch invested ten thousand dollars—their life savings—into opening a pizzeria in Garden City, Michigan. The very first store, located in a strip mall, was called Little Caesars Pizza Treat. The phrase "Pizza! Pizza!," which was originally introduced to promote a buy-one-get-one-free offer, is now synonymous with the chain. The phrase was coined in 1979; according to a company representative, 86 percent of Americans now associate it

The "Deep! Deep! Dish" pizza at Little Caesars.
PR Newswire

- Americans eat three hundred fifty slices of pizza per second.
- Mozzarella is the top-selling cheese variety, followed by cheddar.
- Pepperoni is America's favorite pizza topping, followed by mushrooms and onions. The least favorite is anchovies.
- Nearly 3 million southern Italians entered the United States through Ellis Island from 1880 to 1920.
- As of September 2013, U.S. pizza sales topped $37 billion, with the top three chains (Pizza Hut, Domino's, and Papa John's) accounting for roughly 30 percent of those sales.
- Connecticut boasts the highest percentage of mom-and-pop pizzerias, while Kansas has the highest percentage of chains.
- Roughly 53 percent of all pizza stores are independently owned. The rest are chains with ten or more stores.
- New Hampshire has the highest number of pizza stores per capita, while Hawaii has the lowest.
- World pizza sales in 2013 were estimated at $132 billion, according to Euromonitor International.
- The number of pizzerias in America grew from five hundred in 1934 to twenty thousand in 1956.

Vintage pizzeria menus make fun collectibles.

"PIZZA PRINCE"
PH. 842-3565
CULVER, INDIANA

"IT'S A PRINCE OF A PIZZA!"

PIZZA

	10"	14"
Cheese	.95	1.90
Sausage	1.25	2.30
Pepperoni	1.25	2.30
Mushroom	1.25	2.30
Anchovies	12.5	2.30
Onion	1.15	2.10
Green Peppers	1.15	2.10
Combination	1.40	2.55
Deluxe	1.65	2.80

SANDWICHES

	Half	Whole
Submarine	.60	1.15
Stromboli	.60	1.15
Ham & Cheese	.60	

ADDITIONAL ITEMS

Garlic Bread	.15
Salads	.45
Spaghetti (carry out)	1.05
Spaghetti (Dinner includes garlic bread & salad)	1.50
Milk	.15
Coffee	.10

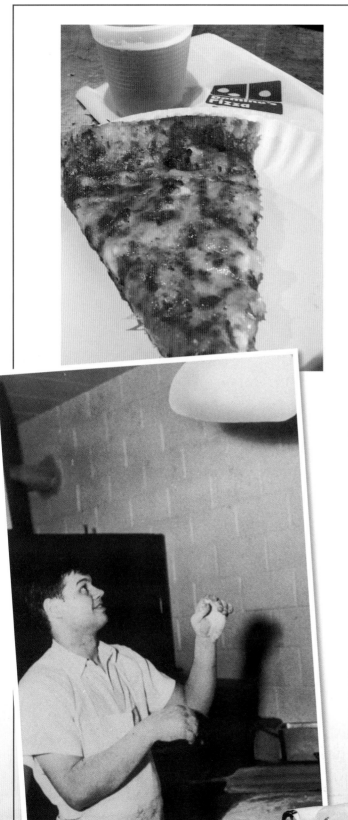

with Little Caesars. Charitable giving has always been a large part of the corporate culture at Little Caesars, with one of its biggest initiatives being the Love Kitchen, a mobile kitchen that provides food to those in need. The chain, with an estimated 3,725 U.S. units, is now the fourth-largest pizza chain in the country.

Domino's entered the picture in 1960, when brothers Tom and James Monaghan purchased an existing pizzeria called DomiNick's in Ypsilanti, Michigan. (The owner gave them a quick pizza-making lesson before they opened.) After only a few months, James decided he wasn't interested in the pizza business and traded his half of the company to Tom in exchange for a Volkswagen Beetle. By 1965, Tom had changed the name to Domino's Pizza. He started franchising two years later. The original logo had three dots on the domino to represent each of the company's stores, and the plan was to add a dot with each new store. That plan, obviously, did not pan out.

LEFT: Tom Monaghan, Domino's co-founder (and future Detroit Tigers owner) in 1965. *Times & Life Pictures / Getty Images* RIGHT: A Domino's car, 1962. *Photo courtesy Domino's*

The company's big break came when Domino's began focusing on delivering pizza, mainly to college campuses in the beginning. They promised that if the pizzas were not delivered in thirty minutes or less, they were free. To this day, Domino's is still referred to as the chain that delivers in thirty minutes or less, despite the fact that the promotion ended in 1993. Tom made the decision to sell Domino's to Bain Capital in 1998. The company has continued to grow and remains the number two pizza chain in America, with 4,928 stores nationwide.

Papa John's, while a latecomer to the chain game, having been founded in 1984, grew rapidly right out of the gate. When founder John Schnatter (who worked in a pizzeria in high school) was still a recent college graduate, he sold his 1971 Camaro in order to purchase the pizza equipment, which he then installed in the back of his dad's tavern in Jefferson, Indiana. His idea was to set himself apart by delivering high-quality pizza with better ingredients. In 2002, Papa John's beat Pizza Hut and Domino's in the digital race by becoming the first pizzeria to offer online ordering nationwide to its customers. There are now 3,131 Papa John's locations across the United States, making it the third-largest pizza chain in America.

While some traditionalists may shun the chains, their impact on the growth of the industry—and their innovations in delivery and online ordering, which ultimately trickle down to smaller pizzerias—cannot be ignored. There will always be an audience for both the big chains and the small, independently owned pizzerias, each filling a specific niche in our growing pizza culture.

Even Subway wants a piece of the pie.

The little plastic item that resembles a tiny table and is often found sitting on top of your pizza inside the box, to prevent it from being smashed, is called a **PIZZA SAVER**.

ABOVE: By the 1970s, pizza practically radiated high-tech energy. *Photo courtesy Jordan L. Smith, The Pie Shops Collection*

CHAPTER FIFTEEN

PIZZA GOES HIGH-TECH

For the first fifty years or so that pizza existed in America, it was fairly low-tech. But just as there was experimentation with pizza ingredients and toppings, additional innovations began to take shape—particularly in the form of technology that promised to help pizza businesses grow.

The first innovation that took pizza to the next level had to be delivery. For the first time, you didn't have to leave your home or office to eat the pizza you loved. While several small pizza places were making deliveries in the 1950s, Domino's Pizza gets the credit for bringing delivery to the forefront, by making it the main focus of its business in the 1960s. Domino's was also the first to use the thermal delivery bag, invented by Ingrid Kosar specifically for the pizza industry in the early 1980s.

Cotrillo's

FEATURING
DRIVE-THRU SERVICE

631-0234

4611 Genesee St.
Near Buffalo International Airport
(adjacent to Beef & Sirloin)
HOURS:
Sunday-Thursday – 10:30 AM to 12 Midnight
Friday & Saturday – 10:30 AM to 1:00 AM

147

Drive-through pizza, a precursor to high-tech pizza.

EXTRA TOPPING

The world's first pizza box dates back to the eighteenth century. The cylindrical copper *stufa* was a metal vessel used to carry pizzas around the streets of Naples, and was often held on the vendor's head. In 1966, Domino's—which at that point had only four stores—introduced modern pizza boxes to America.

Since then, delivery has further progressed, thanks to technological advances such as online ordering, mobile phone ordering, and apps. Texts were able to be sent via cell phones in the early 1990s, but mobile advertising, still fairly rare, didn't start showing up for pizzerias until around 2007. Today, we have the luxury of one-touch pizza ordering via our cell phones.

Online ordering has been available for restaurants since around 2000, but with carryout and phone orders engrained in our consciousness, and with slow computers to boot, it didn't take off right away. A few years later, we've jumped on the high-speed Internet highway, become attached at the hip to our mobile phones, and grown quite obsessed with maintaining an online presence. Online ordering is

© digitallife / Alamy

EXTRA TOPPING

Some pizzerias forego pizza boxes for bags, using a round piece of corrugated cardboard and a thin paper bag that allows the steam to escape.

"The pizza could be as popular a snack as the hamburger if Americans knew about it."

—Jane Nickerson,
New York Times, May 25, 1947

now the norm, with most pizzerias offering it just to keep up with demand. Because ordering is available through Facebook and via apps, some pizzerias have even stopped listing their phone number on marketing materials.

For pizzerias, it helps that online order averages are usually higher, as more time is available to peruse menus, errors are kept to a minimum, and pizzeria staff members are not tethered to the phone all day. The big three chains—Pizza Hut, Domino's, and Papa John's—all set the benchmarks for online ordering records and innovations, opening the door for smaller pizzerias to introduce the technology to their customers.

Point of Sale (POS) systems, those nifty computers that allow restaurants to punch a few buttons and send your order to the kitchen, were first used in retail and grocery settings, before making it to fast-food chains and smaller restaurants. One in three pizzeria operators was using a POS system in 2001. That number has grown to one in two today with the addition of online ordering capabilities, customer tracking, loyalty card programs, and more. POS systems offer a wealth of information and capabilities for the small business owner.

In 2007, nearly 50 percent of consumers said they would use **customer-activated ordering** and **self-serve kiosk payment** terminals if they were available at their favorite dine-in restaurant. Surprisingly, despite this high number, we have not seen many pay-at-the-table terminals in pizzerias, perhaps because many pizzeria operators would like to continue to promote a homestyle, family atmosphere, which can be threatened when too much technology enters the picture.

Food pushcarts date back to the seventeenth century, whereas the **food trucks** we know today can be traced back to the first kitchen on wheels:

the chuck wagon. Rancher Charles Goodnight designed a mobile kitchen for a long cattle drive back in 1866; the cowboys used the slang word "chuck" to mean good food. Mobile food trucks, or "roach coaches," have been around for decades, serving construction workers and others who work in industrial neighborhoods. They were never given much notice until the recession hit, construction work diminished, and chefs were laid off. There was suddenly a surplus of trucks and high-end chefs. The setup cost was minimal for chefs looking to get back into cooking. Pair that with low-to-no cost social media advertising, and the food truck boom was born. Food trucks have now become a $1 billion business, with more pizzerias joining every day.

Quick Response (QR) codes were introduced in 2010, allowing a customer to use a cell phone to scan a square barcode, which would instantly connect to a location on the Internet, such as a

Valducci's Original Pizza truck serves lunch in Greenwich Village, New York. Some popular food trucks Tweet their location. *Richard Levine / Alamy*

There are people who love pizza so much they give tours of pizzerias to other people who love pizza! These folks include Scott Wiener of Scott's Pizza Tours in New York, Jon Porter of Chicago Pizza Tours in Chicago, Tony Muia of A Slice of Brooklyn in Brooklyn, and Theresa Nemetz of Milwaukee Food & City Tours.

pizzeria's menu, online ordering page, map, or special promotion. The codes went from nonexistent to plastered on everything from boxes to billboards, although they are still few and far between in most pizzeria settings.

Increased mobile phone use introduced the pizza industry to additional promotion via **online review sites and blogs**. This was often a double-edged sword, both bringing additional press and giving everyone a public arena to post reviews of all sorts. Ultimately, social media (in the form of Facebook, Twitter, and blogs) has helped to spread news about new and great pizzerias, further expanding pizza's reach and resulting in material for today's endless supply of "Best Pizzerias in America" lists.

Innovation continues to spread throughout the industry, helping to make pizza bigger, better, and faster in the eyes of consumers, pizzeria operators, and manufacturers. America was built on innovation, so it's only natural that pizza would participate.

Our appetite for pizza is as big as this pie, nearly thirty thousand pounds, a record-breaker in 1987. *Associated Press*

ABOVE: Garlic knots at Max's Coal Over Pizzeria in Atlanta.

PIZZA'S PERFECT PAIRINGS

There are some items that just go hand in hand (pun intended) with pizza. When you think of one, you naturally think of the other. What's a football game without pizza and wings, right? Most of the foods that go best with pizza are those that can also be held in our hands, since there aren't usually many forks around when pizza is on the menu.

153

WINGS

In 1964, Teressa Bellisimo took an item that's normally thrown away or used in soup stock and created something that has since become one of America's favorite finger foods. There are several stories on how it came about, but the most common one is that Teressa, who owned the Anchor Bar in Buffalo, New York, with her husband Frank, was about to make some chicken stock when her son Dominic and some friends came to the bar seeking a

The Anchor Bar, where the brilliant coupling began. © *Philip Scalia / Alamy*

snack. Improvising, she threw the chicken wings under the broiler and added some hot sauce. (The wings we know today are deep-fried, then tossed in a sauce made of melted butter and hot sauce.)

Others started copying the Anchor Bar, and chicken wings began to spread to other bars and restaurants throughout Buffalo, New York, in the 1960s and 1970s. But not much was really written about them in cookbooks or in the press. In 1983, the Hooter's chain opened, featuring wings on the menu—which helped them gain further fans. By the late 1980s, most people had either tasted wings or read about them.

However, it wasn't until the early 1990s that pizzerias really started getting into the wing game. Pizza Hut felt confident enough to put wings on

ABOVE: Pizza Hut has almost 4,000 Wing Street locations nationwide. © Ian Dagnall / Alamy

The most popular wings accompaniment is celery.

EXTRA TOPPING

The top five busiest days of the year for a pizzeria are Halloween, the night before Thanksgiving, New Year's Eve, New Year's Day, and Super Bowl Sunday.

Papa John's sold more than nine hundred thousand pizzas on Super Bowl Sunday in 2008, the year it became the "official pizza sponsor" of the NFL. *Associated Press* / Akron Beacon Journal, *Ed Suba, Jr.*

its menu, and when it did, the orders flooded in. The pizza chain did so well with wings that it began WingStreet in 2003, a wing restaurant now attached to almost four thousand Pizza Hut stores nationwide. Meanwhile, another chicken wing entrepreneur, Joey Todaro III of La Nova Wings, was busy selling wings out of his Buffalo, New York, office to the mom-and-pop pizza shops that were clamoring for them. Since then, chicken wings have become one of the most popular sides to order with pizza. The availability of different sauces, ranging from spicy to sweet, can make them downright irresistible.

Pizza has always been, and continues to be, a food designed to be quick and economical. The same can be said for the sides that accompany it. Chicken wings are one of the most economical parts of the chicken, and all the other sides made in a pizzeria are typically made from items that are already on hand.

TOP: Sweet and savory knots at Tour de Pizza in St. Petersburg, Florida.
BOTTOM: Fried cheese goes perfectly with pizza.

CHEESE STICKS

Breaded cheese sticks are decadently delicious, especially when paired with a bowl of warm marinara. I bet you would never have guessed that they've been around since the fourteenth century—a recipe for *pipefarces* (stuffed straws) was found in the book *Le*

Ménagier de Paris, published in 1393.

Fried mozzarella, popular in Italy, was featured in the 1948 Italian movie *The Bicycle Thief*. And the original cheese lovers, the Swiss, were also

Tony Pizzi of Pizzi's Café celebrates pizza
pairings, 1935. Courtesy Pizzi Cafe

making it. So when did we start seeing fried mozzarella in American restaurants? These easy-to-make appetizers (just cheese rolled in bread crumbs and fried) started becoming popular in the early 1970s, and were all over the place by the 1980s. You can still find them on the menus of many pizzerias. Some even feature different cheeses, such as pepper jack, to update the offering.

GARLIC KNOTS

One of my favorite pizza sides is garlic knots. However, these garlic-laden gems can be difficult to find outside of New York or New Jersey. They're made by taking strips of dough, tying them into knots, baking them, then tossing them into a mixture of olive oil, corn oil, garlic salt (or chopped garlic), and Romano cheese. They're usually sold in batches of three or given away as a side with pizza. Garlic knots first started showing up in Long Island, New York, pizzerias in the early 1980s. Unfortunately, their reach hasn't really expanded much, except in instances where a New Yorker opens a pizzeria in another part of the country and adds them to the menu.

Garlic knots are made using leftover dough, while mozzarella sticks use extra cheese not used on the pizzas. You

TOP: Beer and pizza . . . pizza wedding cake, that is (in Idaho, 1968). *Photo courtesy Jordan L. Smith—The Pie Shops Collection*
BOTTOM: The Italian aperitif soda Sanbitter is great over ice or mixed in a cocktail alongside pizza.

> **"Without question, the greatest invention in the history of mankind is beer. Oh, I grant you that the wheel was also a fine invention, but the wheel does not go nearly as well with pizza."** —Dave Barry

may not even notice all the ways that a pizzeria repurposes dough, cheese, and toppings to create interesting appetizers, but that's just part of the magic of a pizzeria.

BEVERAGES

While the idea of pairing food with wine and beer is not new, the trend has really picked up steam in recent years, as pizzeria operators have seen how popular alcohol and food pairings can be with customers. In the same way that pizzerias design specialty pizzas to take the guesswork out of ordering, they're also now helping you decide which beverages will taste the best with the pie you choose. Some host a pairing night once a month, while others include pairing suggestions alongside pizzas on the menu.

Sal & Mookie's in Jackson, Mississippi, regularly holds sold-out beer pairing dinners in which they present five courses, each paired with a different beer from a local brewery. Bertucci's, with locations throughout the Northeast, created a custom beer pairing menu by working hand in hand with Samuel Adams to choose brews that would pair well with specific pizzas. Flying Pie Pizzaria in Boise, Idaho, lists a beer and wine suggestion next to every pizza on its menu, and Frasca Pizzeria + Wine Bar in Chicago offers build-your-own wine flights.

CALZONES

Calzones are cleverly disguised as something new, when in reality they are simply pizzas folded in half and pinched together. Filled with

ingredients ranging from ricotta and mozzarella to meats and veggies, these portable pockets of gooey goodness are perfect alongside a bowl of warm marinara. They're the ideal accompaniment to a salad or an Italian-style soup.

STROMBOLIS

Often confused with calzones, traditional strombolis are made with Italian bread dough that is wrapped around Italian meats and cheeses in a log shape and baked like a sandwich. Nazzereno "Nat" Romano of Romano's Pizzeria & Italian Restaurant in Essington, Pennsylvania, invented the stromboli in 1950. His friend William Schofield suggested that he name the creation after a 1950 movie of the same name, starring Ingrid Bergman.

Strombolis can be found in pizzerias across the nation, and while most are

Stromboli. *Ahturner / Shutterstock.com*

tasty, they usually use pizza dough instead of the traditional Italian bread dough that Romano's uses. This has elicited much confusion over the difference between a calzone and a stromboli.

ITALIAN DESSERTS

Okay, so maybe dessert isn't technically a "pairing," but when you're out with friends and family enjoying a round of pizzas, why not cap off the evening with a cup of cappuccino and a shared tiramisu or gelato? There's no better way to end an Italian meal than with an Italian dessert.

Tiramisu was invented during the 1970s at Le Beccherie, a popular Italian eatery that operated from 1939 to 2014 in Treviso, Italy. The owner's mother, Ada, created the dessert in an effort to provide herself with an energy boost after she gave birth to her son. As you know, there's a good dose of caffeine in tiramisu, as it's made of ladyfingers dipped in espresso and layered with mascarpone. A slice of this along with a cup of Joe will give you a nice caffeine buzz after your favorite pie.

When it comes to gelato, because of the rich, creamy taste of Italy's version of ice cream, many think that the dreamy treat is higher in fat than American ice cream. Not so. In fact, while American ice cream can contain upward of 20 percent butterfat, gelato usually contains less than 10 percent. The reason gelato tastes so creamy is that it contains no air and less ice, and it is served at a slightly warmer temperature than ice cream. Because of these factors, gelato is able to melt on the tongue faster and deliver its flavors immediately.

Pizza is clearly magnificent on its own, with no need for accompaniment. But when faced with so many choices, it's easy to say yes to indulgence every once in a while.

The cappuccino and tiramisu at Fratelli la Bufala in Miami Beach, Florida.

TOP: Pizza encourages exercise! © *GoodSportHD / Alamy*
LEFT: Salmon and Dill Flatbread. *Courtesy SkinnyMommy.com*

PIZZA AND THE DIET REVOLUTION

There was a time, long, long ago, when diets did not exist. In fact, up until a couple hundred years ago, only the rich were overweight, and everyone else had to struggle just to keep meat on their bones. However, once food became plentiful, it was hard to resist, leading to overeating and weight gain. Can you really blame us after starving for so long?

Unfortunately for pizza, it has probably suffered the most when it comes to the diet revolution. The first thing out of most people's mouths when they go on a diet is, "No more pizza!" The tricky part is, when you try to give up something that you love and have been eating your entire life, it's not easy.

I'm always the first person to tell someone that it's about moderation, not restriction. Many friends have heard my speech about how pizza is not inherently bad for you—it's what you put on the pizza. A mega-meats pan pizza with double cheese and crusts dipped in garlic butter will make you fat. Period. A thin-crust pizza with cheese and vegetables, eaten in moderation, is perfectly fine for anyone trying to maintain, or possibly even lose, weight.

Cauliflower, zucchini, and tomato pizza.
MShev / Shutterstock.com

LEFT: A low-carb pizza on display at an industry trade show, with pita bread for the crust. *Associated Press* BELOW: Bacon and cheese are okay on the Atkins diet (hold the pizza crust). *Photo courtesy Jordan L. Smith, The Pie Shops Collection*

In 1862, the first diet book, *Letter on Corpulence Addressed to the Public*, was published in England. The author, William Banting, wrote about the weight-loss success he achieved by following his doctor's orders to restrict sugars and starches (marking one of the first well-publicized low-carb diets). While some doubted his approach, the diet spread nonetheless, as popular diets are prone to do. Many other weight-loss theories followed, including a high fiber method and a process that involved chewing food thirty-two times.

The 1960s and 1970s saw the introduction of the Atkins diet (low carb), the Pritikin principle (low fat, high fiber), and Weight Watchers (low everything). And who could forget the Hollywood diet, cabbage soup diet, Paleolithic diet, South Beach diet . . . . The list goes on. Over the years, we've also seen new diet restrictions enter the picture or take a more prominent role, such as vegetarianism, veganism, gluten intolerance, and lactose intolerance. Pizzerias have attempted to keep up with diet trends and diet restrictions, in an effort to cater to everyone who still wants to eat pizza, even when their conscience may tell them not to.

Low-carb diets were introduced in 1972 with the best-selling book *Dr. Atkins' Diet Revolution*, and reintroduced in 1992 with the updated *Dr. Atkins' New Diet Revolution*. The diet didn't really catch on until around 2000, when millions of people started figuratively tossing loaves of bread into the streets, and eating eggs and bacon with reckless abandon. But there was something missing. Pizza. Flour companies started to see a decline, as 50 percent of the population admitted to trying—though not necessarily sticking to—the Atkins diet. Even one of pizza's favorite beverage pairings, beer, was suffering. Michelob introduced Michelob Ultra, with fewer carbs, to appease those who were giving up beer.

Pizzerias had to do something to bring customers back. Thankfully, even those who were enjoying a diet that let them have cheeseburgers sans buns and cheesy steak tacos wrapped in lettuce still missed going to their favorite pizzeria. The answer came in the form of low-carb versions of pizza, including styles incorporating toppings on low-carb tortillas, Portobello mushrooms, soy flour crusts, and high-protein crusts with whey protein. If all else failed, the toppings could be eaten alone, on a bed of crisped cheese.

Whole-wheat bread, and, in turn, whole-wheat pizza crust, has steadily gained in popularity since the early 2000s. While this type of pizza doesn't necessarily offer much in the way of calorie, carbohydrate, or fat reduction, it plays into the idea of being a healthy alternative to traditional pizza crust.

"There's a pizza place near where I live that sells only slices. In the back you can see a guy tossing a triangle in the air."

—Stephen Wright

The appearance of flatbreads—such as these from Chicago's National Restaurant Association show—has been increasing at industry trade shows.

In the same vein, flatbreads have seen strong and steady growth on pizzeria menus, where they are often paired with salads for a "healthy" meal.

Gluten intolerance is a big deal when it comes to pizza. Those suffering from celiac disease are unable to properly digest gluten, one of the main components of pizza crust, and are dealt a heavy blow when they find out they may have to live a pizza-free future. Doctors have been talking about celiac disease since the early nineteenth century, but it remained unnoticed outside of medical circles. It wasn't until the early 1990s that celiac disease was accepted as an autoimmune condition triggered by gluten. Still, it has only been in the last five years or so that we've really seen the incidence of gluten-free pizzas increase on pizzeria menus.

© Martin Shields / Alamy

"There are two laws in the universe: the law of gravity, and everybody loves Italian food."

—Neil Simon

Initial attempts to create gluten-free breads and pizza crusts were noble, but not always delicious. New recipes that incorporate hearty seeds and wheat-free grains have welcomed celiac sufferers back into the pizza world. However, due to the dangers of cross contamination with regular flour, some pizzerias won't attempt to serve gluten-free pizza. But for those who do, business has increased; loyal fans will travel across state lines to get a taste of the pizza they've been missing from their diets.

The popularity of Meatless Mondays, vegetarian needs, and a general decline in meat consumption over the past decade have inspired many pizzerias to create pizzas that cater to those looking for meat-free options. Remember, when pizza was first introduced, there was no meat topping. The simplicity of a tomato pie with a dusting of cheese was all we ever craved.

It wasn't until 1919 that pepperoni—now America's favorite topping—came on the scene. We likely started seeing

A healthy caprese flatbread from Old Venice Pizza Company in Oxford, Mississippi.

it appear on pizzas shortly thereafter. Italian-Americans were accustomed to dried salamis back home and naturally created a substitute in America, using some of the same methods but with a bit more spice. (You may see dried salamis in upscale Italian eateries, but you hardly ever find pepperoni outside of a pizzeria.) Pepperoni and other meats are an intrinsic part of American pizza culture, and there will always be those who seek a mighty meat pie when they go into a pizzeria. But for others, there are now infinitely more options

Space food has come a long way—a vegan pizza is prepared by NASA scientists. *Associated Press*

when it comes to meat-free specialty pizzas. In some locations—including large chains, such as the Atlanta-based Uncle Maddio's Pizza Joint, which offers tofu and vegan cheese along with standard toppings—there are additional meat substitutes, including tofu, tempeh, and seitan.

One of the most difficult food items for vegans and those with lactose intolerance to give up is cheese. Vegan cheese has been available since the early 1980s, but we first started seeing it show up in pizzerias three or four years ago in response to an increase in veganism. The all-vegan Blackbird Pizzeria in Philadelphia serves a full range of pizzas topped with vegan-friendly proteins and cheeses.

In 1918, a California doctor, Lulu Hunt Peters, published *Diet and Health with a Key to the Calories*, showing, for the first time, the idea of counting calories to lose weight. It wasn't until 1990 that the Nutrition Labeling and Education Act (NLEA) passed, making it a requirement for all packaged foods to carry nutrition labels. We are just now beginning to see calorie counts on pizzeria menus. Whether this will encourage us to make "healthier" decisions remains to be seen. In the meantime, moderation is key to having your pizza and eating it, too.

Matt McClellan

Matt McClellan is the originator of the Pizza Diet and the owner of Tour de Pizza in St. Petersburg, Florida. In 2010, he biked from St. Petersburg to New York, stopping at pizzerias and spreading the healthy-pizza word along the way.

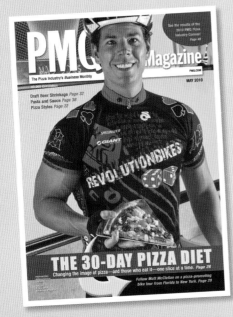

Matt McClellan. *Cover photo courtesy* PMQ *Pizza Magazine; photo by JohnXD*, 24/Seven Magazine

How long have you been in the pizza business?
My first day of business at Fuhgidabowdit Pizzeria in Denver, Colorado, was December 21, 2004. I sold the pizzeria in June 2007, moved to St. Petersburg, Florida, and opened Tour de Pizza in January 2008.

Where did you get the idea to start a diet based on pizza?
The inspiration came from my friend Rob Perry. Business was booming, but I'd go home feeling empty each night. I felt that I was contributing to the unhealthy lifestyles of my customers. Rob Perry was twenty years old and over two hundred and fifty pounds. I wanted to feel good about how I made money, so I committed myself to the idea that my business would help contribute to my customers' nutrition. I told Rob that if he wanted to eat more

than two slices per meal, he had to earn it by working out with me. This became our new routine. After three months, Rob had lost over fifty pounds. Seeing Rob's success, I knew that I had to make it my mission to turn the image of pizza from that of a junk food to a health food.

What are some of the main things people may not realize about the nutritional benefits of pizza?
The tomato sauce on pizza is loaded with lycopene. Lycopene has been proven to fight—and protect you from—certain types of cancer such as prostate, mouth, and lung cancer. Pizza topped with vegetables such as onions, peppers, and olives is a great way to get in essential vitamins and minerals. Throw in some garlic and you get all the benefits of its antibacterial and antimicrobial properties.

Why is pizza something you feel you can eat every day?
From a nutritional standpoint, pizza is a perfect combination of carbohydrates, fats, and protein. You are able to customize it in a way that makes it extremely healthy. Outside of nutrition, pizza is fast and convenient, and it can be found everywhere. Best of all, it's inexpensive.

When going out for pizza, what are the top three healthiest types of pizza, for those watching their weight?
There is the staple of the industry: Margherita pizza, which includes tomatoes, mozzarella cheese, and basil. My second choice would be Neapolitan style, which is a classic. Finally, I would say that if your local pizzeria offers a vegetable-based pizza, that is the one you should go with. The more vegetables, the better. If you do not like vegetables, pizza is the best way to disguise the flavor and make eating healthy more enjoyable.

Pizza in the Movies answers:

1. Screaming heads

2. *Hi, Mom!*

3. Pizza Hut

4. Ordering

5. Because there are no photos of black men displayed in the pizzeria

6. Inappropriately touching himself with his pizza

7. Robbing a bank

8. Dungeons & Dragons

9. L'Antica Pizzeria Da Michele in Naples

10. Sean Penn

11. A mailman

12. Little Nero's Pizza

13. Garbage disposal

14. Señor Pizza, with a sombrero and fake mustache

15. Two

16. Pizza the Hut

17. 42

18. Beer

19. Her ring

20. Pepperoni

BIBLIOGRAPHY

Several pizza makers helped to make this book complete by sharing delicious recipes, and others, such as Scott Wiener of Scott's Pizza Tours, John Arena of Metro Pizza, and Jonathan Porter of Chicago Pizza Tours, graciously offered their time and pizza stories.

I also consulted more formal resources, listed below. This is just a handful of the informative books, periodicals, and websites that are available if you're interested in learning more about America's favorite food. I highly encourage you to continue your exploration using any of the resources listed below. They all go great with pizza.

BOOKS/PERIODICALS

Bonwich, Joe. "Provelology: The Study of a Made-Up Cheese with a Made-Up Name." *St. Louis Post-Dispatch* (St. Louis, MO), May 15, 2012.

Buonassisi, Rosario. *Pizza: From Its Italian Origins to the Modern Table.* Firefly Books, 2000.

Capuzzo, Jill P. "The Original." *New Jersey Monthly Magazine,* January 12, 2010.

Fountain, John. "Ike Sewell, 87, Creator Of `Chicago-Style' Pizza." *Chicago Tribune* (Chicago, IL), August 21, 1990.

Helstosky, Carol. *Pizza: A Global History.* London, UK: Reaktion Books, 2008.

Klieger, Dr. P. Christiaan. *The Fleischmann Yeast Family,* Mount Pleasant, NC: Arcadia Publishing, 2004.

Mariani, John F. "Everybody Likes Italian Food," *American Heritage* (Maryland), December 1989.

Miller, Hannah. "American Pie." *American Heritage* (Maryland), 2006.

Norman, Bud. "No Humble Pie." *The Shocker Magazine (WSU Alumni Magazine),* Fall 2008.

Pollack, Penny and Jeff Ruby. *Everybody Loves Pizza.* Covington, KY: Clerisy Press, 2005.

Rector, Sylvia. "Detroit's Old-School Pizza: It's Hip to be Square." *Detroit Free Press* (Detroit, MI), June 4–10, 2009.

———. "Shortage of Steel Pans Has Detroit-Style Pizza Makers Scrambling." *Detroit Free Press* (Detroit, MI), January 23, 2011.

Reinhart, Peter. *American Pie.* New York: Ten Speed Press, 2003.

Sloane, Julie and Tom Monaghan. "Tom Monaghan Domino's Pizza: The Pioneering Pizza-Delivery Chain I Started Almost Didn't Make It Out of the Oven." *Fortune Small Business Magazine,* September 1, 2003.

Stewart, Jocelyn Y. "California Chef Pioneered Gourmet Pizza Revolution." *Los Angeles Times* (Los Angeles, CA), January 4, 2008.

Turner, Geoff. "Canadian Invented the Hawaiian Pizza." *Toronto Sun* (Toronto, Ontario), July 14, 2010.

Waters, Alice. *Chez Panisse Pasta, Pizza, Calzone.* New York: Random House, 1984.

Wiener, Scott. *Viva La Pizza! The Art of the Pizza Box.* New York: Melville House, 2013.

WEBSITES

ChefTalk.com, www.cheftalk.com
Culinary Schools, www.culinaryschools.com
Encyclopedia of Chicago, www.encyclopedia.chicagohistory.org
Food Editorials, www.foodeditorials.com
Frank Pepe's Family Owned Restaurants, www.pepespizzeria.com
History, www.history.com
International Dairy Foods Association, www.idfa.org
Mozzarella Company, www.mozzarellaco.com
Passion-4-Pizza.com, www.passion-4-pizza.com
Pizza Making, www.pizzamaking.com
Pizza Napoletanismo, www.pizzanapoletanismo.com
Pizza Quest with Peter Reinhart, www.fornobravo.com/pizzaquest
PMQ Pizza Magazine, www.pmq.com
RoadFood.com, www.roadfood.com
Scott's Pizza Tours, blog.scottspizzatours.com
Serious Eats, www.slice.seriouseats.com
St. Louis Post-Dispatch, www.stltoday.com
The Daily Meal, www.thedailymeal.com
The Food Timeline, www.foodtimeline.org
The Herb Society of America, www.herbsociety.org
The Pizza Insider, thepizzainsider.pmq.com
TheHistoryOf.net, www.thehistoryof.net/
What's Cooking America, www.whatscookingamerica.net
Wisconsin Milk Marketing Board, www.eatwisconsincheese.com

Pizza goes for a spin before getting sliced at Coletta's Restaurant in Memphis.

Photograph by Benjy Foster

ABOUT THE AUTHOR

Liz Barrett is the former editor-in-chief and current editor-at-large of *PMQ Pizza Magazine*, the number one pizza industry magazine in America. She also maintains *PMQ*'s The Pizza Insider, a weekly blog focusing on pizza industry topics. Her award-winning website EatingOxford.com has been covering the restaurant industry in and around Oxford, Mississippi, since 2009.